INFORMATION COLLECTION:
THE KEY TO DATA-BASED DECISION MAKING

Paula M. Short

Rick Jay Short

Kenneth Brinson, Jr.

EYE ON EDUCATION
6 Depot Way West, Suite 106
Larchmont, NY 10538

ISBN 1-883001-46-3

Library of Congress Cataloging-in-Publication Data

Short, Paula M.
    Information collection : the key to data-based decision making /
Paula M. Short, Rick Jay Short, Kenneth Brinson, Jnr.
        p.   cm. -- (School leadership library)
    Includes bibliographical references.
    ISBN 1-883001-46-3
    1. Education--United States--Information services. 2. Information
storage and retrieval systems--Education--United States. 3. School
management and organization--United States--Decision-making.
4. School principals--United States.   I. Short, Rick Jay.
II. Brinson, Kenneth, 1961-   . III. Title. IV. Series.
LB1028.27.U6S46   1998
025.06'37--dc21
                                                        97-31186
                                                            CIP

The School Leadership Library:

Information Collection
by Paula Short, Rick Jay Short, and Kenneth Brinson, Jr.

Instruction and the Learning Environment
by James W. Keefe and John M. Jenkins

Interpersonal Sensitivity
by John R. Hoyle and Harry M. Crenshaw

Judgment: Making the Right Calls
by Jim Sweeney and Diana Bourisaw

Leadership: A Relevant and Realistic Goal for Principals
by Gary M. Crow, L. Joseph Matthews, and Lloyd E. McCleary

Motivating Others: Creating the Conditions
by David P. Thompson

Oral and Nonverbal Expression
by Ivan Muse

Organizational Oversight:
Planning and Scheduling for Effectiveness
by David A. Erlandson, Peggy L. Stark, and Sharon M. Ward

Problem Analysis: Responding to School Complexity
by Charles M. Achilles, John S. Reynolds, and Susan H. Achilles

Resource Allocation
by M. Scott Norton and Larry K. Kelly

Student Guidance and Development
by Mary Ann Ward and Dode Worsham

Written Expression: The Principal's Survival Guide
by India Podsen, Glenn Pethel, and John Waide

If you would like information about how to become a member of
the **School Leadership Library**, please contact:

Eye On Education
6 Depot Way Suite 106
Larchmont, N.Y. 10538
(914) 833-0551 Phone
(914) 833-0761 Fax

ABOUT THE AUTHORS

Paula M. Short, a former building and district level administrator, is currently Department Chair and Professor of Educational Leadership and Policy Analysis at the University of Missouri-Columbia. Dr. Short has published extensively in the area of school empowerment, including the *School Participant Empowerment Scale*, and her recent book, *Leadership in Empowered Schools: Themes from Innovative Efforts*. She has published over 50 articles in leading educational journals and has co-authored two recently published books, *School Principals* and *Change and Rethinking Discipline: Alternatives that Work*. She is the editor of the *Journal of School Leadership*. In 1993 she received the NASSP Distinguished Service Award at the Assessment and Development Center Director's annual meeting and has served on the NAESP Committee to revise two documents, *Standard for Principals* and *Standards for Elementary and Middle Schools*. She is a member of the Technical Advisory Committee to ETS for the Interstate School Leaders Licensure Consortium.

Rick Jay Short is the Director of the School Psychology Training Program, Director of the Center for Learning, Evaluation, and Assessment Research (CLEAR), and Associate Professor of Educational and Counseling Psychology at the University of Missouri-Columbia. He also served as an Assistant Executive Director for Education in the American Psychological Association in Washington, DC. He has published numerous articles on assessment and psychological services for children and adolescents in leading journals and has authored books and book chapters on assessment, prevention of substance abuse and delinquency, and service delivery.

Kenneth H. Brinson, Jr. served as a teacher, coach, and school administrator before assuming a position as Assistant Professor of Educational Leadership and Foundations at The University of Texas at El Paso. He is a contributing editor for the Pennsylvania School Study Council's quarterly publication, *The Beacon* and serves on the board of directors for the New England Educational Research Organization, Inc. He has done frequent research and consulting work for the Center for Total Quality Schools and the Pennsylvania Superintendent Leadership Development Program.

ACKNOWLEDGMENTS

Fred Aderhold, Principal of John F. Kennedy Elementary School in Sioux Falls, South Dakota

James Doud, University of Florida

Nancy Evers, University of Cincinnati

Phillip F. Flaherty, Principal of Westwood Elementary High School in Westwood, Massachusetts

John F. Gilbert, Principal of Oaks Middle School in North Miami Beach, Florida

Maria Luisa Gonzalez, New Mexico State University

Tim LaValley, Principal of Barnard Central School in Barnard, Vermont

Jody Lehr, Forman University

Linda Saukkonen, Principal of Clear Springs Elementary School in Minnetonka, Minnesota

Penny Smith, University of North Carolina at Greensboro

James R. Thompson, Principal of Wolcott Street School in LeRoy, New York

Patricia J. Robertson, Seattle, Washington

Myra L. Walker-Sims, Seattle, Washington

The National Association of Elementary School Principals

The National Association of Secondary School Principals

The International Alliance of Invitational Education

FOREWORD

The School Leadership Library was designed to show practicing and aspiring principals what they should know and be able to do to be effective leaders of their schools. The books in this series were written to answer the question, "How can we improve our schools by improving the effectiveness of our principals?"

Success in the principalship, like in other professions, requires mastery of a knowledge and skills base. One of the goals of the National Policy Board for Educational Administration (sponsored by NAESP, NASSP, AASA, ASCD, NCPEA, UCEA, and other professional organizations) was to define and organize that knowledge and skill base. The result of our efforts was the development of a set of 21 "domains," building blocks representing the core understanding and capabilities required of successful principals.

The 21 domains of knowledge and skills are organized under four broad areas: Functional, Programmatic, Interpersonal, and Contextual. They are as follows:

FUNCTIONAL DOMAINS
  Leadership
  Information Collection
  Problem Analysis
  Judgment
  Organizational Oversight
  Implementation
  Delegation

PROGRAMMATIC DOMAINS
  Instruction and the Learning
    Environment
  Curriculum Design
  Student Guidance and
    Development
  Staff Development
  Measurement and Evaluation
  Resource Allocation

INTERPERSONAL DOMAINS
  Motivating Others
  Interpersonal Sensitivity
  Oral and Nonverbal
    Expression
  Written Expression

CONTEXTUAL DOMAINS
  Philosophical and Cultural
    Values
  Legal and Regulatory Applications
  Policy and Political Influences
  Public Relations

These domains are not discrete, separate entities. Rather, they evolved only for the purpose of providing manageable descriptions of essential content and practice so as to better understand the entire complex role of the principalship. Because human behavior comes in "bunches" rather than neat packages, they are also overlapping pieces of a complex puzzle. Consider the domains as converging streams of behavior that spill over one another's banks but that all contribute to the total reservoir of knowledge and skills required of today's principals.

The School Leadership Library was established by General Editors David Erlandson and Al Wilson to provide a broad examination of the content and skills in all of the domains. The authors of each volume in this series offer concrete and realistic illustrations and examples, along with reflective exercises. You will find their work to be of exceptional merit, illustrating with insight the depth and interconnectedness of the domains. This series provides the fullest, most contemporary, and most useful information available for the preparation and professional development of principals.

Scott D. Thomson
Executive Secretary
National Policy Board for
Educational Administration

PREFACE

As the authors note at the beginning of their text: "This is the information society." This single fact has profound implications for the principal. Never before has so much information related to the operation of the school been available, not only to the principal but to the various individuals, offices, and groups that comprise the school and the context in which it functions. Teachers, parents, and community members have access to information about the operation of schools that before was often unavailable to them. Their access to this information has, in many cases, increased their desire to participate in the decision processes of the schools and has, in most cases, enhanced their ability to do so. The principal also has ready access to a wealth of data that previously were not readily available. However, as the amount of accessible information has grown, principals have not always had the skills to analyze and use it. As a result, in recent decades schools have become increasingly rich in the information they collect and store but, at the same time, increasingly poor in their processes of analyzing and applying this information. Principals are often figuratively drowning in a sea of information.

This volume by Paula Short, Rick Short, and Kenneth Brinson methodically explores the information sources that are available to the principal -- both those that currently exist in the schools and those that may be generated. The authors describe the various strategies and procedures for collecting, analyzing, and organizing this information. They emphasize the importance of presenting information in an appropriate format to those audiences who will use and implement it. They demonstrate the value of rich information in identifying potential problems and monitoring progress in the various phases of the school's operation.

Their practical discussions of these processes describe a wide range of tools and opportunities for collecting valuable information, from computers to conversations. They explain the information collection value and practical use of surveys, interviews, questionnaires, and test and measurements. They describe how both qualitative and quantitative data may be collected, organized, and analyzed to provide a foundation for program evaluation and daily decisions. They illustrate how the school staff and parents can be involved and empowered in these processes.

Constantly they re-emphasize the principle that knowledge is power and that information empowers individuals and groups in the service of the school. Information is valuable to the degree that is directed toward practical decisions made by these individuals and groups for implementation of the school program. Numerous case studies and illustrative material makes this principle come alive. Practical direction is provided for principals who would strengthen their information collection skills.

It would not be an overstatement to say that much of a principal's success in the twenty-first century will depend upon his or her ability to collect, analyze, and use the information that surrounds the operation of the school. This short text gives the principal useful, practical advice for strengthening these skills.

David A. Erlandson
Alfred P. Wilson

TABLE OF CONTENTS

1

BUILDING AN UNDERSTANDING OF INFORMATION COLLECTION

LIVING IN THE INFORMATION AND TECHNOLOGICAL AGE

This is the information society. The world's knowledge base has doubled twice during the twentieth century and continues to increase geometrically (Cornish, 1986). Business and industry leaders forecast that current data informational systems will be replaced by ". . . sophisticated devices for knowledge creation, capture, transfer, and use" (Dede, 1989, p. 23). New ways of storing and accessing data make it possible to use information in all types of decision-making activities. In fact, information and the ability to use information have become a strategic resource of the society (McClune, 1985).

In addition, our economy is rapidly becoming globally interdependent, indicating the need for greater knowledge and understanding of world culture (Benjamin, 1989). The population of the United States is becoming more multi-ethnic and multi-cultural, creating increasingly complex value systems that require greater involvement in and understanding of the communities in which people live and work.

Our societal values are shifting from those of the industrial age to values closely aligned with the technology age. For example, we see a movement from competition to cooperation; from isolation to interdependence; and from hierarchical power structures to participative decision making.

The impact of these shifts can be seen in the workplace. There is a growing movement to use teams in the workplace, suggesting that a value is being placed on collective knowledge, skills, and creative energy of groups of individuals. This cooperative teaming enhances the quality and quantity of output in organizations (Peters, 1987). Teams of workers in the workplace increase the creative problem-solving capabilities of the organization. These characteristics will require skills and competencies in critical thinking, reasoning, and creative problem solving. With technology supplying high amounts of knowledge to this workplace, higher-order thinking skills will be necessary to "extract and tailor knowledge from the high information capacity of the tool . . ." (Dede, 1989, 24). One outgrowth of this will be the necessity of schools to help individuals to become lifelong learners, constantly using formal and information mechanisms to meet evolving learning needs. The team structure in the workplace demands workers who can function in a cooperative setting, focusing on group task performance and collaborative learning. Workers will need to be flexible and adaptable to new individuals on the teams. In addition, workers must demonstrate the ability to assume total responsibility for the quality and efficiency of output of the teams. They also will need the ability to engage in the process of learning in order to acquire quickly the skills for new tasks.

Finally, the growing social problems facing young people today will demand that schools look to the wider community for help in solving these dilemmas. Interagency collaboration will be necessary if student needs are to be met. Schools will need to include the community in setting the direction and priorities of the school for framing and solving problems so that all students can learn.

Some notions regarding leadership require that leaders have the knowledge to work with the societal demands affecting schools and to creatively frame and find alternative solutions to the complex problems brought on by ambiguity and conflict (Bridges, 1993). School leaders must be able to use information to make critical decisions on important issues. In addition, principals must be able to build collaborative environments where the collective wisdom of the participants is called upon to establish successful learning experiences for children with increasingly complex needs. Principals must value diverse opinions and multiple perspectives gained through a systematic data-gathering process that produces information from multiple sources.

DECISION MAKING IN ORGANIZATIONS

STRATEGIC PLANNING

Faced with rapid technological and societal advances and a need to deal with organizational transformation, strategic planning provides a method for managing change. Strategic planning involves studying changes in the larger society and the way those changes may impact on the school organization (McClune, 1986). The environment can provide both threats and opportunities for the school organization's effort to deal with change. Institutional capacity is another important dimension of strategic planning and involves evaluating the extent to which the school can build on its strengths in addressing change. The process allows the school to evaluate the match between societal conditions and the school's activities (McClune, 1986). Thus, strategic planning can be described as a method of "identifying issues and decision making" (McClune, 1986, p. 1). If information is a strategic resource, then the primary use of data in decision making becomes critical in dealing with change.

Components of strategic planning, external environmental scanning — threats and opportunities, institutional capacity analysis, planning assumption analysis, goal setting, implementation and assessment — require the collection and use of all types of information from multiple sources. Specifically, types of information that might be obtained in the strategic planning process include the following:

- economic, social, political, and educational trends
- school resources, both present and future

+ human resources, both present and future
+ population trends of the school community
+ stakeholders' opinions and values
+ technological opportunities and needs

Strategic planning requires the involvement and participation of representatives of the population the school serves or may serve in the future. Gathering data regarding their views on the goals and mission of the school is critical to planning success. Linking gathered data to information gathered about societal changes and their implication for education becomes a critical leadership task of the principal.

Four critical areas of data gathering in the strategic planning process include the following (McClune, 1986):

+ External Scanning — the identification of the economic, political, social, and educational trends and their potential impact on schools.
+ Internal Scanning — an evaluation of the effectiveness of the school, including human, fiscal, and programmatic dimensions.
+ Community/School Futures Analysis — providing stakeholders the opportunity to learn about future and present trends prior to assessing their perceptions regarding future direction of the school.
+ Stakeholder Input — an analysis of stakeholders' perceptions through surveys, interviews, seminars, and other data collection avenues.

When data are gathered, they must be analyzed and used in developing a goal and mission statement and developing an understanding of the issues that impact the school organization, and in determining data needed to measure stakeholders' response to the initial set of goals. Critical to the strategic planning process are data that allow the monitoring of the impact and progress of the plan. Plans must be evaluated against changing environmental dimensions as well as trends in organizational capacity. Trend analysis, which requires the maintenance of a database of information, is a powerful and necessary tool for issue management and organizational renewal.

PROGRAM EVALUATION

A critical area for data collection involves program evaluation. Principals must facilitate program evaluation in order to know how well educational programs are meeting the needs of children. An educational program is defined (Medley & McNergney, 1984) as "an enterprise or activity planned to provide those who take part in it with experiences that will produce specific learning outcomes" (p. 180).

Approaches to program evaluation include collecting data on program context, input, process, and product. Program context refers to the activities and decisions prior to the adoption of the program, including need assessment, goal definition, and related activities. Program inputs include (Medley & McNergney, 1984) instructional competencies or skills and knowledge of the teachers. Professional attitudes and values of the teachers would be included under instructional competencies. Additional program inputs include support provided to the program personnel in terms of facilities, instructional material, equipment, supplies, etc. (Medley & McNergney, 1984). Preexisting characteristics of the group of students involved in the program would be considered program inputs (Medley & McNergney, 1984). Student attitudes, aptitudes, interests, socioeconomic status, ethnicity, and other characteristics would be program inputs.

Program processes, those activities that go on during a program operation, are important to assess in program evaluation. Evaluation of program processes is important because of the direct effect they have on program outcomes (Medley & McNergney, 1984).

Program outcomes assume that the program's impact on the learner can be measured in ways that allow one to judge the relative difference the program has made on the student. Program effects can be measured by evaluating the extent to which the program met goals set forth at its initiation. This is called objectives-based evaluation. Another approach to output evaluation is called goal-free evaluation (Medley & McNergney, 1984). Goal-free evaluation takes a "wide-lens" look at the entire program impact, staying open to any findings that may suggest how the program has affected students.

Obviously, a variety of information must be gathered in order to engage in program evaluation. The process of data gathering is influenced by the type of evaluation being conducted as well as the type of educational program being evaluated.

INFORMATION COLLECTION MODEL

Information collection for planning and decision making should be a systematic process for the school principal. While the literature suggests a number of models for data gathering, the document, Principals for Our Changing Schools (Thomson, 1993), presents a distinct eight-step model that makes sense for school needs (see Figure 1.1).

INFORMATION NEEDS

When faced with a decision to be made, the principal must determine if new information is needed and, if so, what that should be. The principal must look to the various inputs from the environment and within the organization for possible data. A critical activity at this step is to determine what information already exists and what new information is needed. Failure to gather the right type of information at this stage will inhibit the ability to make appropriate decisions about a problem or situation. Too little information or the wrong kind of information can cause the principal to incorrectly identify the problems or the causes of the problem. For example, if a school is experiencing an increase in children who require free lunches, it will be important to follow these children regarding their achievement and performance in the school in order to determine if changes are warranted in addressing their learning needs.

FIGURE 1.1. MODEL OF THE INFORMATION COLLECTION PROCESS

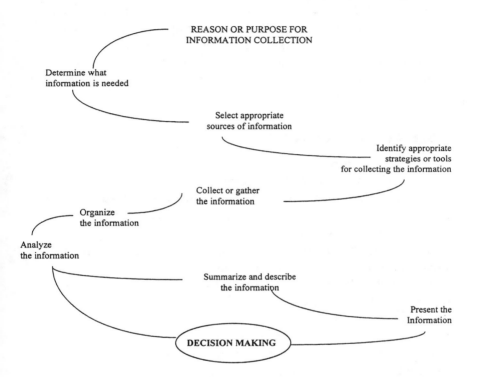

INFORMATION SOURCES

Key activities (Thomson, 1993) of the principal at this stage of data collection include identifying all possible sources of information useful in understanding the problem. Sources useful in past data collection activities might be revisited. Data gathered from multiple sources do provide varying perspectives on issues and problems and are to be encouraged. However, it is critical to recognize the potential for bias from any source. Credibility and political implications must be considered in identifying potential information sources (Thomson, 1993) as well as the relative cost and difficulty in obtaining information from certain sources. For example, a middle school is moving into a more interdisciplinary team teaching approach but is unsure how parents will respond. One source of important data is parents and the extent of their knowledge and understanding of how this teaching approach will change traditional approaches to working with parents. The school can use data from parents to plan strategies for parent education and involvement in programs to get them acquainted with the new approach.

COLLECTION STRATEGIES

The collection step in the information collection model involves decisions regarding the tools and strategies to be used in the actual gathering of data (Thomson, 1993). Based on the information needs, decisions about the types of instruments to be used must be made by the principal. The principal must seek out experts in interviewing, survey and test instrument development, population sampling, and observation scale development to assist in appropriately valid and reliable processes. Key determinants in this step include costs, use of multiple measures, evaluating information sources against needs, and prioritizing strategies relative to time and critical need (Thomson, 1993). For example, a principal wants to get information regarding the climate and culture of the school. The principal must make choices between data-gathering tools and processes that must be purchased from NASSP or another professional association or the use of other sources of data collection that may yield less reliable and valid information but might be less costly.

COLLECTION PROCESS

During this step, actual information is gathered. The principal must ensure that people involved in the gathering of data are trained to administer the instruments to be used in the data collection. Observations and interviews should be conducted during this step. Focus group interviews are useful with students and groups of parents and community leaders at this stage. The principal must facilitate and manage this process with a clear understanding of the types of data being collected and for what reasons. Quality control during this phase of the process is critical. For example, a principal of a middle school wants to conduct a needs assessment on technology. Does she contract with researchers at a local university with expertise in technology to collect the data or does she organize teachers and/or parents in the school to collect the data?

INFORMATION ORGANIZATION

Information gathered from instruments, observations, surveys, focus group discussions, and mail surveys must be organized for analysis purposes. Databases are extremely useful at this stage in helping to organize, classify, and store data being gathered. One of the critical tasks of the principal is to find ways of organizing data in databases that make retrieval simple and useful. Many principals use commercial databases that organize information into certain categories useful in decision making.

INFORMATION ANALYSIS

The critical step in the process involves taking the data collected and analyzing it for trends, patterns, and significant findings (Thomson, 1993). Data from all sources must be used in identifying these patterns of relationships that inform the problem-framing and problem-solving activity of the principal. Linking categories of findings in ways that inform the cause of the problem is important. Data may be narrative as well as numerical. For example, a principal may collect data on school climate and culture and analyze it for patterns of teacher concerns, student issues, and administrative issues. On the other hand, the principal may simply want to analyze the data looking for the most important and critical issues overall.

INFORMATION SUMMARIZATION

Important in the data collection model are developing strategies for portraying and communicating findings from the analysis of the data. Transforming findings into tables, graphs, diagrams, and statistical tables will be helpful in drawing conclusions about findings as well as communicating those findings to stakeholders and other audiences (Thomson, 1993). Narrative summaries also are important in illustrating data that are supportive of findings.

INFORMATION PRESENTATION

When presenting findings from the data-collection process, it is important that the appropriate mode of communication be chosen for a particular audience (Thomson, 1993). Characteristics of the various audiences will dictate the type of detail and mode of illustration chosen for communicating findings. Obviously, effective oral and written communication is imperative (Thomson, 1993).

Principals need to understand the importance of information to their decision making. Principals develop unique strategies to collect information on a formal and informal basis. It is instructive to see how three principals approach information collection on an ongoing basis to assist them in their decisions. The following mini-cases illustrate those approaches. We asked three powerful school leaders to reflect on their overall use of information in their work. In some cases, their responses address the model. In other cases, their reflections indicate their sincere desire to acquire and use information in their work.

MINI-CASES

MARY LAFFEY

Mary, an award-winning middle school principal in Columbia, Missouri, has developed specific strategies for gathering information used in decision making. She uses both formal and informal means for gathering the information important to effective action. She recounts some of her strategies are as follows:

1. An open door policy for a flow of information based on a relationship of trust between myself, teachers, and the supportstaff.
2. Monthly faculty council and faculty meetings. The faculty council is an elected representative group of teachers who meet monthly with the principal to go over school policies and issues. Information flows to this committee anonymously. No sources are ever identified in the flow of information. This channel allows teachers an opportunity to voice concerns and have them heard by the faculty. While I still hold the ultimate decision-making power based on the faculty's input following a discussion, I personally can't remember a time in the last nine years when I have overridden one of the faculty council's decisions. These faculty councils are then followed by general faculty meetings that involve the entire faculty.
3. A review of weekly procedures with personnel to coordinate our efforts. Weekly staff meetings with guidance and other administrative personnel in the building to review the upcoming week and what to expect.
4. Monthly PTA Executive Board Meetings.
5. Attendance at all school events. This particular strategy allows me an opportunity to be accessible to parents for informal discussions.

Being available and accessible are two essential components of being able to receive information. This role becomes increasingly difficult as the demands of the principalship continue to expand, but accurate and up-to-date information is essential for progress to be made in the name of good education for children.

JOHN THOMPSON

John R. Thompson, dynamic principal of Wolcott Street School in LeRoy, New York, presents an interesting perspective on information needs. He relates what he considers important ways for gaining information:

The principalship tends to be a lonely job at times and it is most important to find ways to gain greater insight to handle ever-increasing challenges. Communicating with administrators and other educators on-line has proven to be one of the most exciting ways to share ideas, exchange strategies, gain insight into effective programming, and even share a laugh or two! Let me give some specific examples of how and where this takes place using America On-Line: I host a National Distinguished Principal's (NDP) Chat on AOL one Sunday evening a month. Anywhere from 15-25 principals (several of them National Distinguished Principals) and other educators show up each month to exchange and share ideas and interact with my "guest of the month." My guests this past year have included: Dr. Mary Lee Fitzgerald, Director of Princeton's Principal's Center; Professor Bill Silky, Professor of Educational Administration from SUNY Oswego who has written a great deal on the impact of shared decision making on pupil achievement; and Dr. Kathy Kelbs-Corley, who is putting together a "break the mold school" for the State of Massachusetts.

I participate in two other monthly principal's chats through the National Principal's Center (sponsored by NAESP). George Manthey, a California elementary school principal, hosts these chats and coordinates the National Principal's Center.

Through the National Principal's Center on AOL there is an extensive idea and message exchange on a wide variety of topics!

I have dozens of educational e-mail friends across the country. On an almost daily basis I correspond with: technology directors from Texas, New Mexico, and Florida; fellow principals in Pennsylvania, New York, Massachusetts, Georgia, California, Missouri, etc.; noted authorities on Multiple Intelligence and Constructivist Education; math specialist on the NCTM Standards; language arts specialists from across the country, etc. etc...!

I have an ongoing e-mail communication with a principal who is putting together a break the mold school in Salem, Massachusetts. We communicate several times a week and exchange that all-important "craft knowledge" that Roland Barth talks about in Improving Schools from Within.

Just last evening I participated in the first "Educational Chat" sponsored by the Orlando Sentinel Newspaper on AOL. Twenty-six educators showed up for the first chat and I will be leading the discussion in three weeks focusing in on Improving Schools from Within.

At the NAESP National Convention at San Diego, I made a presentation at the National Distinguished Principal's Reunion meeting (I am the '94 NDP from NYS) about the potential of getting on-line and sharing craft knowledge. Together with George Manthey, we hope to present at the '96 NAESP National Convention in Washington, DC, with an interactive on-line chat linking up with principals from across the country on-line.

I have made the proposal to NAESP that I could be available at the NDP Award Ceremony in October to introduce each NDP Class to on-line communications and try to enlist or recruit members of that NDP class to join our on-line conversations.

On the state level, I have recently communicated with SAANYS (State Administrators' Association in New York State) about putting together on-line/e-mail capabilities for the state's membership to share ideas, craft knowledge, etc.

I have found on-line communication expands my knowledge exponentially. Ongoing sharing of information with fellow principals and practitioners gives me access to tremendous amounts of information and insights from across the country which results in better decision making.

GINGER HOVENIC

Ginger Hovenic, outstanding principal of Clear View Charter School in Chula Vista, California, has an interesting story about her school's approach to data collection.

Clear View School took an interesting and unique approach to data collection this year, one which I am sure will yield valuable data in the future. We first assembled the school demographics:

1. Number of students and grade levels
2. Ethnic breakdown
3. Level of English
4. Socioeconomic status (reduced or free lunch or welfare)
5. Educational program: Regular Ed, GATE, RSP, SDC
6. Student mobility
7. Attendance records

This is all information routinely reported by the District Office. We then looked at the goals of our educational program that we could standardize and measure. Our focus became:

- Grades K-3
- Literacy — fluency in reading and writing
- Mathematical competency — problem-solving, mathematical concepts
- Grades 4-6
- Critical reading and writing
- In-depth problem-solving, concepts, and mathematical creativity

Portfolios illustrate each student's progress as a reader and writer. They are a continuing source of reference and reflection for each student, as well as a valuable tool for conducting student-led conferences with teachers and parents. Students begin assembling their portfolios from the first week of school. Past efforts have yielded a concrete Scope and Sequence for Language Arts Portfolios. In the 1995-96 school year, we will formalize a similar Scope and Sequence for Math Portfolios.

Beyond portfolios, school administration, staff, parents, and community need to look more broadly at performance trends. To enable us to do this, the following procedure evolved: To illustrate our goals for students in Language Arts and Math, each teacher assembled class data on a uniform spreadsheet via networked IBM computers. For each student, demographic items 2-5 were used. Individual data were added throughout the year as follows:

GRADE DATA COLLECTED

- Kindergarten — Letter or sound identification, number sense, oral language fluency
- Grades 1-3 — Pre-and post-holistic writing scores
- Running Record (oral reading fluency) 3 times per year
- Stanford Achievement Test (Reading Comp/Math Conc) Grade 3
- Grades 4-6 — Pre- and post-holistic writing scores
- Marginalia (reading comprehension) 3 times per year
- Integrated Assessment test
- SAT — previous year's and current year's scores

In the spring, when all data had been assembled, focus groups were conducted. We randomly chose 2-5 students who reflected particular demographics of the school, as well as parents who met similar criteria. We talked informally, eliciting information about our programs, homework, class assignments, reporting to parents, compliments, and concerns. This gave both life and depth to the data we collected.

Sorts of who-school data were then performed by demographic items 2-5. Next year, we plan to expand to include items 6 and 7. Sorted results were examined to identify strengths and problem areas on which we need to focus. Results were also cross-referenced with SAT and California Learning Assessment test results. Parent and student information yielded data that we used to measure attitude and self-esteem issue.

APPLICATION ACTIVITIES

1. Assess the types of data you currently collect on an annual basis and reflect on data that might be important to add to your annual collection.

2. Discuss with teachers in your school the types of relevant data that they would find useful if collected.
3. Ask three fellow principals in other districts how they use certain types of information in decision making regarding particular parent issues, community concerns, student achievement, and school effectiveness.
4. Reflect on the principals in the mini-cases and their use of information. Do you note a trend in all three cases regarding data use and importance? What role does the need for communication play in their reflections on the collection of information in their work?

REFERENCES

Benjamin, S. (1986). An ideascape for education: What futurists recommend. Educational Leadership, 47 (1), 8-12.

Bridges, E. (1993). The prospective principals; program at Stanford University. In J. Murphy (Ed.), Preparing tomorrow's school leaders: Alternative designs. University Park, PA: University Council for Educational Administration.

Cornish, E. (1986). Educating children for the 21st century. Curriculum Review, 25(4), 12-17.

Dede, C. (1989). The evolution of information technology: Implications for curriculum. Educational Leadership, 47(1), 23-16.

McClune, S. D. (1986). Policy issues: State strategic planning. Charleston, WV: Appalachia Educational Laboratory.

Medley, D. M. and McNergney, R. F. (1984). Program evaluation. In J. Cooper (Ed.), Developing skills for instructional supervision. New York: Longman.

Peters, T. (1987). Thriving on chaos: Handbook for a management revolution. New York: Knopf.

Thomson, S. (1983). Principals for our changing schools. Fairfax, VA: National Policy Board for Educational Administration.

2

THE "WHAT" AND "WHERE" OF INFORMATION COLLECTION

One of the key activities for principals in the information collection process is determining what information is needed and selecting the appropriate sourses for that information. Some of the key concerns regarding information gathering include (1) prioritizing the types of information needed, (2) categorizing available information, (3) anticipating the consequences of using certain types of information, and (4) prioritizing the sources of available information.

PRIORITIZING TYPES OF INFORMATION

Principals live in an environment that is rich in information. Local and state regulations require that certain types of data be gathered and maintained throughout the school year. Data on children, teachers, parents, and the community can be sources of information useful in strategic planning, problem solving, goal setting, school improvement efforts, and reporting to the public regarding the status of education. The issue for the school principal is to determine what information is important in what situation. Some data may be more critical than others depending on their intended use. As is often the case, critical data for a particular issue, and therefore high-priority information, are often not gathered on a systematic basis so those data must be obtained. This can be a challenge to the principal.

CATEGORIZING AVAILABLE INFORMATION

While there is information that is readily available to principals, it is important to know how that information can inform the decision-making process. Information must be categorized in such a way that it is useful in dealing with specific types of issues that arise in the school environment. Data on student dropouts, disciplinary referrals, achievement, and student employment outside the school might be useful in understanding how effective the school is in meeting the needs of all its students.

ANTICIPATING CONSEQUENCES

While information can be most useful in decision making and problem solving in schools, certain information can present problems that must be anticipated. The act of gathering data from students, teachers, parents, and the community can uncover a level of distrust among these parties and the school. The reporting of certain types of data to the public can cause alarm and misinterpretation of the data. For instance, reporting student test results on state-mandated achievement tests by race and gender can create many problems. Obviously, this type of reporting can lead to polarizing of populations and labeling of groups that are not in the best interest of children. Principals must be aware of the consequences of such reporting.

PRIORITIZING SOURCES OF INFORMATION

For information to be useful to the principal, it is necessary to place a priority on the most critical sources of data for principal decision making and problem solving. For example, if the middle school finds itself being criticized because there are no guards at school crosswalks, then it may be important to gather data on student use of the crosswalks, potential for student accidents at the crosswalk (frequency of cars, number of students using the crosswalk, any unreported incidents of problems, parent perception of the need for a guard at the crosswalk, etc.). If the city police department makes the decision regarding the assignment of police at school crosswalks, then these data are critical in making a decision to present a case to the policymakers for a guard. A principal cannot simply assume that junior high kids are old enough to get across a street by themselves. These become priority data to gather before a serious accident occurs.

It is helpful to present illustrations of principals who understand the need to identify types of useful data, the need to categorize the data, the importance of anticipating the possible consequences of the use of certain types of data, and the need to prioritize the sources of important data. The two cases presented next provide insight into this important issue. One case explores how a school addressed the needs of a particular group of students through data collection and data use. The second case illustrates how a principal utilized data and a specific data collection strategy to gauge teacher perceptions of empowerment. In addition, her use of those data provides an interesting way to grow and change as a school leader as she worked to become a more empowering principal.

CASE STUDY ONE

This most critical aspect of information collection will determine the quality of data collected in terms of their usefulness and effectiveness. One elementary school in Seattle, Washington, recognized the critical nature of gathering appropriate information to address a specific need in the school. The principal, John Morefield, and faculty at Hawthorne Elementary School wanted to improve the way they worked with bilingual children and their families in meeting the needs of these children. They felt that a needs assessment would be the appropriate first step to take in problem solving and making decisions about how to better address the needs of this particular group. Patricia J. Robertson was an administrative intern in the Danforth Principal Preparation Program at the University of Washington working at Hawthorne Elementary School. Patricia has agreed to let us tell the story in her words of how one school effectively determined the "what" and "where" of information collection in an attempt to find out how to better work with a significant group of children and parents in its school community. Patricia's story follows:

In January 1995, one Seattle public elementary school began a process to try to improve its connection to families of bilingual children in attendance there, and to help them to become more knowledgeable about the school culture. This article will discuss how the process to conduct a needs assessment of the bilingual community at Hawthorne Elementary School came about, what we learned from the experience, and outcomes for enhanced involvement of non-English-speaking parents in their children's education.

Of the total population of approximately 500 students at Hawthorne Elementary School in Seattle's south end, about 80 are students of Limited English Proficiency (LEP). These students may or may not have been born in this country, but because they speak a language other than English at home, they begin school with a language limitation that their native-English-speaking peers do not have to face. They are served by the ESL classes that are offered at Hawthorne and a number of other "Bilingual Center Schools" throughout the district, and the expectation is that within five years, with the extra help, they will have the facility they need to master the regular school curriculum. This is the goal, but in reality many Seattle students spend more time than this in special ESL classes, especially at the secondary level, because their standardized test scores do not reflect sufficient improvement for them to become ineligible.

The parents of the LEP students are recent immigrants, themselves burdened by little English fluency, and typically not very involved with the school. They come to this country with cultural experiences of schooling and parenting that may be very different from mainstream American society, and because their interaction with others is limited, they often find that their expectations and current experiences conflict. Our efforts at Hawthorne were aimed at breaking down some of the barriers to interaction.

Since its inception seven years ago, this school has had a dynamic and well-organized parent group, the Friends of Hawthorne (FOH). The FOH has sponsored events for the children, raised funds, written grants, and provided volunteer help in and out of the classroom. After organizing a welcoming event at the school in the fall of 1993, several of the parents noticed that bilingual families were conspicuous by their absence, and set about planning ways to increase the school's contacts with those families.

It was in keeping with the spirit of inclusiveness in the ethnically diverse school that the impetus for the process came from the parent community. Myra Walker-Sims and Bee Lim, both members of the Welcoming Committee, are active participants in the life of the school, and their sense of empowerment led them to wonder about the limited involvement of LEP parents. What were the concerns of bilingual parents in regard to their children's education? How well did they understand school programs and services that were offered? What were the ways the school might better serve their needs? Walker-Sims, a Hawthorne parent who serves as co-chair of that committee, was adamant that the voices of the parents of the LEP students be heard. "Too often we make assumptions, because their ability to communicate their interests is limited. We might be right about some of those assumptions, but we need to let them speak to find out if that's true."

Contact was made with Cam Do Won, a multilingual and multicultural specialist who works with the Refugee Women's Alliance (ReWA) in Seattle. Ms. Wong suggested that a Needs Assessment be done with the bilingual families, and the Hawthorne Welcoming Committee began planning based on her experience and ideas. With a corps of trained bilingual families, Ms. Wong had been involved in an event in another school district designed to assess the needs of the bilingual community there. The same sort of event was planned for the Hawthorne families: an international dinner to be followed by a meeting, using interpreters, to discuss issues of concern.

FIGURE 2.1. BILINGUAL FAMILY SURVEY
HAWTHORNE ELEMENTARY SCHOOL

You are a part of the Hawthorne family and we want to hear from you. This information will help us to better understand and meet the needs of you and your children. Please complete the form — circle yes or no, or check where appropriate. If you prefer, you may respond to the survey in your home language. Please have your child return this form to school by Monday, March 20th. Thank you.

1. Here is a list of programs and services we offer. Please check the ones you are familiar with:

___ Hawthorne Happenings   ___ Chess Club
___ Reading is Fundamental   ___ Site Council
___ Health & Nutrition Dinner   ___ Computer Lab
___ Mom's Clothes & Food Closet (Family Room)
___ Friends of Hawthorne
___ Young Author's Committee

If you or your child have not attended any of the programs or used the services, please check the reasons why:

___ Childcare   ___ Time   ___ Transportation
Other reason (s) _____

PLEASE CIRCLE YES OR NO FOR THE FOLLOWING QUESTIONS:

2. Are the programs and services helpful to you?
    Yes   No

3. Are the programs and services helpful to your child?
    Yes   No

4. Do you have any concerns regarding these programs and
    services?
    Yes   No

If you marked yes, what are your concerns?

_____

_____

5. Do you feel comfortable coming into the school?
    Yes   No

6. Have you had an opportunity to meet with the following?
   (Please check):
   ___ Your child's teacher
   ___ Principal John Morefield
   ___ Other parents
   ___ Bilingual staff member(s)

7. Have you spent time in your child's classroom?
   Yes   No

8. If you have not spent time in your child's classroom, please check
   reason(s) why:
   ___ Language barrier
   ___ I have small children
   ___ I work during the day
   ___ I don't know how I could help
   ___ Other reason (s) _____

9. Did you attend the parent/teacher conference?
   Yes   No

10. Do you understand the discipline techniques and policies?
    Yes   No

    Do you have any concerns?
    Yes   No

    If you marked yes, what are your concerns?
    _____
    _____

** Think about programs or services you would like to see at Hawthorne.
Bring these ideas with you at the April 4th International Potluck to be
discussed.

NAME _____ Phone # _____
___ I Will Attend   ___ I'm Unable to Attend
___ Number of Adult Members Attending
___ Number of Children Attending
___ Childcare Needed   ___ Transportation Needed

** PLEASE HAVE YOUR CHILD RETURN THIS FORM TO THE
SCHOOL OFFICE BY MARCH 20TH!! THANK YOU.

THE NEEDS ASSESSMENT

A needs assessment was considered a critical element in the Seattle neighborhood from which the bilingual population of Hawthorne School is drawn; it is multicultural and multilingual, unlike some communities that have a dominant culture or language group. Where such diversity exists, the possibility of simply offering a bilingual experience for adults and children is complicated. No ESL teacher can be expected to speak all of the languages represented at Hawthorne, so the emphasis is by necessity on curricula that crosses cultures, and not on developing literacy in the native language before attempting to develop skills in English. Any services which were to be offered to the community would have to be multilingual in nature.

EARLY AND INCLUSIVE PLANNING

It was important to leave ample lead time to involve all families who would want to be included. We obtained a list of those students who were served by the ESL program, and their families were sent a letter of invitation a month before the event, along with a questionnaire designed to elicit what they knew and thought about school programs.

One parent on the welcoming committee, herself a native speaker of a language other than English, observed that some children may be fluent enough in English not to need ESL classes, but their parents may not speak English. We were made aware through her observation that these parents would be as limited in their communication with the school as those whose children were identified as participants in the ESL program. By asking a few questions of those children who were identified by school staff as having parents who were bilingual — "What language do your parents speak at home? Do your parents speak English also?" — we were able to ascertain which of those families should also be a part of the needs assessment survey, and to ensure that they received an invitation to the dinner.

THE QUESTIONNAIRE

The letter of invitation and information questionnaire, compiled by Myra Walker-Sims, were translated for the language groups for which we had bilingual staff and volunteer parents.   Of 63 questionnaires distributed, 38 (60%) were returned, giving us some ideas about the focus for questions to be posed at the dinner meeting. As expected, the language groups for which we had no translation services had the lowest response rate.

STAFF INVOLVEMENT

Our next task was to involve the school staff responsible for the ESL program at the school, while trying not to increase their workload dramatically. One teacher of ESL commented early in our planning that she hated to sound cynical, but international dinners similar to this one that she had planned over many years of teaching had not been well-attended by bilingual parents. So, following the suggestions of Cam Wong, we embarked on an aggressive "sell job" to try to ensure a good turnout.

Hawthorne is fortunate to have three very talented and professional multilingual instructional assistants (IAs) who speak several languages and dialects. Through them we were able to have the letters and questionnaires translated for Cambodian, Vietnamese, Chinese, Laotian, and Mien families. We asked a teacher on staff who was fluent in Spanish to do the same for that language. We did not have written translation services available for the remaining languages, which included Tagalog and Iiocano (Filipino languages), so these were sent out in English. One multilingual parent agreed to conduct phone surveys for the five families from Ethiopia and Sudan.

Though this event was aimed at connecting with the bilingual families in the school, we were careful to make it clear that the entire school staff, not just the ESL staff, was encouraged to attend. An announcement at a staff meeting, and written invitations in the mailboxes of each teacher and all other school staff, were reminders that their presence was important to

establishing two-way communication. However, staff attendance at the dinner was disappointing to the parent planners.
The bilingual staff and ESL teachers attended, as did a few of
the other teachers. Perhaps the sense that this was not an "all-
school event" was the reason for the non-involvement of the
majority of the staff. I reflected afterward that popping into
classrooms at the end of the day and extending a personal face-
to-face invitation might have elicited a higher turnout.

PERSONAL TELEPHONE INVITATIONS

As Cam Wong indicated, her experience revealed that
bilingual parents would be most likely to attend an event of
this type when extended a personal invitation. First of all,
there was no guarantee that the parents to whom letters were
sent were literate even in their own language, so a phone call
beforehand was the only guarantee that they would all be
made aware of the event. The bilingual IA's were tireless in
their efforts to personally contact every family whose languages they spoke. Relaying the information orally made a
significant difference, as the turnout was greatest among those
groups who received a call from school personnel or one of the
other parents. We were unable to find a speaker of Tagalog or
Iiocano, and asked at the last minute for assistance from one
of the ReWA interpreters. But none of the Filipino families
came to the dinner/meeting, and we wondered if the lack of
direct contact from a school staff member might have been the
reason.

CULTURAL NORMS

It is important to be sensitive to cultural differences in
preparing for an event of this type. We determined, in discussion with the bilingual staff and some of the parents, that the
concept of "potluck" is not familiar to many of the groups
involved. Though we encouraged families to bring a dish representative of their country of origin to share, we did not
expect that all would do so. Food was provided by the school,
and staff was encouraged to contribute as well. We also took

into consideration the fact that many of the bilingual families, as refugees, have few resources.

We were also advised by our bilingual IA's that parents from a number of these ethnic groups are not likely to plan a long time in advance to attend such an event and mark a calendar to remember to come. So a reminder call was made to each family one or two days before, extending an invitation once again. When asked at the meeting what were the main elements in their decision to attend, parents cited this personal contact as being a key factor. We were very pleased with the final count of approximately 130 people in attendance, including adults and children. About 45 of those were bilingual parents.

SOCIAL GATHERING OR MEETING?

We wanted to emphasize that the purpose of this event was twofold: it was to get school personnel and bilingual families together for a celebration of our rich multicultrual diversity, and also to establish some lines of communication so that they would have a chance to express their opinions and attitudes. The dinner was a way for us to interact socially and informally, children had an opportunity to introduce their parents to Principal John Morefield and to their teachers, and all participants enjoyed the various ethnic dishes provided. Most of the social interaction took place within language groups, of course, because of the restrictions automatically placed on communication among those who do not speak one another's language. But with the help of the bilingual translators present, some conversation took place among the teachers and their students' parents.

When dinner was over, children were excused to the childcare room, and adults were asked to join groups of other speakers of their language, where interpreters would facilitate their participation in the meeting. Cam Wong conducted the discussion by posing to the group as a whole some general questions that had arisen from the questionnaire returns. Individual language groups then discussed and recorded their responses to the questions:

1. What kind of challenges and concerns do you have about your children and the school?
2. What kind of programs would you like to see Hawthorne provide for your family?
3. How can the school get the parents more involved?
4. What needs do you have and what special services would you like to see the school provide?

Following small-group discussion, the responses were shared with the assemblage as a whole, allowing time for interpreters to translate to their groups. This sharing process was necessarily quite time-consuming, but it helped the groups to see where they had the same concerns and interests.

CHILD CARE AND TRANSPORTATION

Provision of child care was a must for this type of event. The questionnaires revealed that a major reason for parent non-participation in school events was the presence of young children in the home. Making the dinner a family affair, and providing child care during the meeting, ensured a greater turnout. We were lucky to have parent volunteers from among the FOH who looked after the children in one of the classrooms while parents met in the cafeteria.

Though we had planned to provide bus transportation for families, it did not prove necessary. Few of the families indicated a need for transportation, so instead we encouraged carpooling in our phone invitations. For those who needed it, several staff members offered to give rides. On the returned questionnaires, transportation was listed by only three families as the main reason for their non-involvement in school activities, whereas lack of child care and insufficient time were more significant factors.

INTERPRETERS

Providing interpreters was critical to the success of the meeting. LEP parents often indicate that they would be more apt to come to school events and participate in their child's classroom activities, but they are frustrated when they think that they will not be understood. Interpreters made it possible for parents to explain in some detail their concerns and opinions about the school. The interpreters for this event were hired as trained facilitators, but upon reflection the committee decided that the school's bilingual IA's were capable of serving this function for at least some the language groups represented.

FOLLOW-UP

From the results of the questionnaire and the answers to questions posed at the dinner meeting, reports were compiled by Myra Walker-Sims, co-chair of the FOH Welcoming Committee. The report summaries provided a basis for proceeding with suggestions to undertake on-going activities which might enhance involvement of LEP families in the school. The committee met with the bilingual staff, and the result of their discussion was a plan to contact Seattle Community College about the possibility of offering ESL classes at Hawthorne for the LEP parents.

Another on-going project which resulted from the general meeting is the continued networking among the parents in specific language groups. Already some of those groups have met to discuss their own unique interest, and their mutual support of one another should help to break down some of the barriers to communication that were felt before.

CASE STUDY TWO

Karrie White, principal at Longwood Junior High School, has been concerned for several years about the extent to which teachers in the school felt empowered. She had begun an effort to change the culture of the school when she became the new principal. She valued shared decision making and teacher opportunities to grow and develop professionally in the school. She wanted to be an empowering leader.

Karrie was very aware that the former principal had run a very authoritarian office and most teachers had long given up any idea of a collaborative, collegial relationship as professionals. Karrie began immediately to work on building trust among the teachers and to establish processes that gave teachers a voice in critical decisions in the school. After several years' effort at rebuilding a collaborative environment, Karrie felt it was important to gather information regarding teachers' perceptions of the changing environment in support of empowerment. Karrie wanted to know if teachers felt that they were empowered at all.

Karrie discovered an instrument that met her needs. The School Participant Empowerment Scale (SPES) was distributed in a statewide meeting of the Leadership Academy to several teachers in Longwood Junior High School. One of those teachers brought the instrument to Karrie's office. Karrie liked the instrument because it allowed her to assess teacher empowerment in six areas: (1) teacher level of involvement in decision making, (2) teacher sense of autonomy, (3) teacher belief that they were having an impact, (4) teacher sense of status in the school, (5) teacher sense of self-efficacy, and (6) the extent to which teachers felt that their school afforded them the opportunities to grow and development professionally. The School Participant Empowerment Scale (Short & Rinehart, 1991) follows:

FIGURE 2.2. SCHOOL PARTICIPANT EMPOWERMENT SCALE
© PAULA M. SHORT AND JAMES S. RINEHART

Please rate the following statements in terms of how well they describe how you feel. Rate each statement on the following scale:.

1= Strongly Disagree
2= Disagree
3= Neutral
4= Agree
5= Strongly Agree

1) I am given the responsibility to monitor programs.   1 2 3 4 5
2) I function in a professional environment.   1 2 3 4 5
3) I believe that I have earned respect.   1 2 3 4 5
4) I believe that I am helping kids become independent learners.   1 2 3 4 5
5) I have control over daily schedules.   1 2 3 4 5
6) I believe that I have the ability to get things done.   1 2 3 4 5
7) I make decisions about the implementation of new programs in the school.   1 2 3 4 5
8) I am treated as a professional.   1 2 3 4 5
9) I believe that I am very effective.   1 2 3 4 5
10) I believe that I am empowering students.   1 2 3 4 5
11) I am able to teach as I choose.   1 2 3 4 5
12) I participate in staff development.   1 2 3 4 5
13) I make decisions about the selection of other teachers for my school.   1 2 3 4 5
14) I have the opportunity for professional growth.   1 2 3 4 5
15) I have the respect of my colleagues.   1 2 3 4 5
16) I feel that I am involved in an important program for children.   1 2 3 4 5
17) I have the freedom to make decisions on what is taught.   1 2 3 4 5
18) I believe that I am having an impact.   1 2 3 4 5

19) I am involved in school budget decisions.   1 2 3 4 5
20) I work at a school where kids come first.   1 2 3 4 5
21) I have the support and respect of my
    colleagues.   1 2 3 4 5
22) I see students learn.   1 2 3 4 5
23) I make decisions about curriculum.   1 2 3 4 5
24) I am a decision maker.   1 2 3 4 5
25) I am given the opportunity to teach other
    teachers.   1 2 3 4 5
26) I am given the opportunity to continue
    learning.   1 2 3 4 5
27) I have a strong knowledge base in the areas
    in which I teach.   1 2 3 4 5
28) I believe that I have the opportunity to grow
    by working daily with students.   1 2 3 4 5
29) I perceive that I have the opportunity to
    influence others.   1 2 3 4 5
30) I can determine my own schedule.   1 2 3 4 5
31) I have the opportunity to collaborate with
    other teachers in my school.   1 2 3 4 5
32) I perceive that I making a difference.   1 2 3 4 5
33) Principals, other teachers, and school personnel
    solicit my advice.   1 2 3 4 5
34) I believe that I am good at what I do.   1 2 3 4 5
35) I can plan my own schedule.   1 2 3 4 5
36) I perceive that I have an impact on other
    teachers and students.   1 2 3 4 5
37) My advice is solicited by others.   1 2 3 4 5
38) I have an opportunity to teach other teachers
    about innovative ideas.   1 2 3 4 5

Karrie knew that simply administering the instrument to the entire faculty and then analyzing the results herself would not be very empowering to the faculty. After much thought, she decided to send a copy of the instrument with a personal note to each teacher asking them, if they wished, to complete the instrument, calculate a mean for each of the six areas of empowerment that the instrument measured, reflect on the results, and then set up a time to meet with her regarding any areas in which the calculated mean fell below 3.0. (The SPES uses a five-point Likert-type scale with anchors of (1) strongly disagree to (5) strongly agree.) The discussion and dialogue that followed provided a way to generate collaboration with each teacher that gave direction for Karrie to make necessary changes that were disempowereing to individual teachers.

As teachers met individually with Karrie regarding their reflections on the information gathered with the instrument, Karrie gained insight into specific areas where she, as principal, should make changes in order to help teachers feel a better sense of empowerment. She and the teachers determined, as a collaborative group, what processes and structures should change in order to give teachers greater autonomy, choice, and opportunities to share expertise.

While this was a voluntary activity for teachers in Karrie's school, the results have demonstrated that teachers can self-assess their own level of empowerment and then work with the principal to find ways to address problems. Because Karrie knew what information should be gathered and combined it with a very empowering strategy for teachers for data collection, she has information that is critical in her attempts to become a more empowering leader.

APPLICATION ACTIVITIES

1. Identify a special issue you are concerned about in your school and reflect on the types of data that, if collected, might give you insight into that issue.
2. How might you use the School Participant Empowerment Scale in your school?
3. Conduct an inventory of information available to you from the community and reflect on how it might be used to improve your school.

REFERENCES

Short, P. M., and Rinehart, J. S. (1991). School Participant Empowerment Scale.

Walker-Sims, M. (1995). A needs assessment for non-English speaking families of Hawthorne Elementary School. Unpublished manuscript.

3

THE "HOW" OF INFORMATION COLLECTION

After determining what information is needed and identifying germane sources of that information, the educational
practitioner turns to the "How" of information collection. This
process centers around strategies for gathering information
and the selection of tools or instruments to gather data effi-
ciently and successfully. Due to the particular strengths and
weaknesses of varying strategies, one must consider the para-
meters of the individual situation. What are the constraints of
cost, time, potential for bias, and ease of collection? What is
the perceived exactitude of the information to be gathered?
Which strategies offer the best value, given these constraints,
for the current investigation? Which strategies will help
achieve the desired outcomes?

KEY CONCERNS

The primary concern of the building level practitioner
should be to identify as many strategies for the collection of
information as can be ascertained. Next, one should turn to
acknowledged sources of information, such as test scores and

file data, that are already available. Then, the reliability and the validity of established measuring procedures should be evaluated and interpreted. All information collection strategies being considered should then be analyzed against the specific information needs and acknowledged sources. The culmination of this effort is to rank-order, or prioritize, those strategies deemed most applicable to the present circumstances. This ranking should take into account the costs, time, potential for bias, and ease of collection involved, as well as the perceived adequacy of the information collected. By prioritizing or ranking the strategies, it should be easier to select those that will be utilized.

IDENTIFYING STRATEGIES

In identifying various strategies that might be suitable for a particular situation, the process must be driven by the situation being investigated. Does the situation demand quantifiable evidence? Are opinions and observations of participants more fitting with the needs of the situation? The sources of information that have been identified also necessarily influence the procedures to be chosen. The Joint Committee on Standards for Educational Evaluation (1981) suggests acquiring enough measures of information to do comparisons on the information they yield (p. 112). Table 3.1, Information Collection Procedures, provides several measures that might

FIGURE 3.1. FACTORS THAT IMPINGE ON INFORMATION GATHERING PROCEDURES

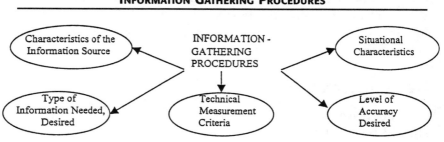

be acquired in order to do comparisons of information. What factors can alter the assortment of strategies in this first step? Stufflebeam and his associates (1985) suggest several factors in the following figure and further suggest that each be given due consideration "since disproportionate attention to any one may tend to violate another" (p.87).

Those factors must be ever-present in the mind of the administrator during the scrutiny of potential strategies to ensure the selection of favorable instruments. Characteristics of the information source pertain to the individual situation and background of those with the sought-after information. The effect those characteristics can have include not only the procedure chosen, but the manner in which information can be retrieved, whether it must be compensated, and problems that may be associated with the sources' particular situation. Situational characteristics that should be evaluated include costs, timing, environment, political implications, and ethical considerations.

John F. Gilbert, Principal of Highland Oaks Middle School in North Miami Beach, Florida, has found weekly staff meetings to be critical in his quest for information. In a letter to the authors, he wrote "by gathering administrative staff at the beginning of each week, I am able to keep everyone, including myself, aware of the activities, meetings, and events scheduled. . . I also use this time to review current personnel, curriculum, budget, faculty, and community issues with staff." It is important to remember that some of the best sources of information may be at the practitioners' fingertips.

L. R. Gay (1992) suggests three data collection methods for use in educational research that may serve as guidelines:

(1) administer a standardized instrument

(2) administer a self-developed instrument, or

(3) record naturally available data (such as grade point averages and absenteeism rates) (p. 152)

There are numerous methods that might be utilized. In choosing between them it is helpful to have a basic understanding of what each is essentially designed to do. On the surface, no one procedure is necessarily superior, but their

FIGURE 3.2. INFORMATION COLLECTION PROCEDURES

Procedure	What It Measures, Records	Example
Case Studies	The experiences and characteristics of selected persons in a project or program.	Several special education referrals are tracked throughout the relevant diagnostic sources to illustrate how parents are involved and react to these procedures.
Interviews (group or individual)	Persons' responses and views	Teachers interview pupils about school attitudes.
Panels, hearing	Opinions, ideas	A panel of teachers reviews the needs assessment survey data to give interpretations.
Records analysis	Records, files, receipts	Resource center files are analyzed to detect trends in material used.
Logs	Behavior and reactions are recorded narratively.	Teachers maintain a log of disciplinary actions with pupils.
Simulations	People's behaviors in simulated settings	Teachers are videotaped conducting a simulated diagnostic session.
Sociograms	Preferences for friends, work, and social relationships	An IEP committee reviews their interactions during meetings.
Systems analysis	Components and subcomponents and their functional interdependencies are defined	The payroll and accounts payable processes in a school business office are depicted by a flow chart.
Advisory, advocate teams	The ideas and viewpoints of selected persons	Teams are convened to debate the merit of two competing in-service plans.

Information Collection Procedures (Continued)

Procedure	Description	Example
Judicial review	Opinions in the context of a systematic review of relevant information	A "jury" of teachers review the data collected on a pilot program to decide if it should be adopted throughout an entire district.
Behavior observation checklist	Particular physical and verbal behaviors and actions	Record how frequently teachers use a new questioning technique.
Interaction analysis	Verbal behaviors and interactions	Observers code teacher-pupil interaction.
Inventory checklist	Tangible objects are checked or counted	School bulletin boards are checked for in-service-related materials.
Judgmental ratings	Respondents' ratings of quality, efforts, etc.	Experts rate the adequacy of the school's curriculum and schedule.
Knowledge tests	Knowledge and cognitive skills	Faculty are tested on knowledge of state education laws.
Opinion survey	Opinions and attitudes	Superintendents are asked to rate their attitudes toward collective bargaining.
Performance test and analysis	Job-related and specific task behaviors	Principals are observed and rated n how they conduct an interview.
Delphi technique	Group consensus	Teachers' inservice committee reaches consensus on program goals.
Self-rating	Respondents rate their own knowledge or abilities	Teachers rate how well they can administer different diagnostic devices.
Survey questionnaire	Demographic characteristics, self-reported variable	Teachers report how frequently they use certain resource center materials.
Time series analysis	Data on selected variable are compared at several time points	Frequencies of key pupil behaviors are charted over the course of a new reading program.
Q sort	Self-reported attitudes	Administrators are asked to complete a Q-Sort regarding many aspects of educating disabled students.

Note: Sometimes these procedures can be "quantified," that is, categories can be established using numerical codes, so that numerical data are produced.

applicability to the situation at hand may determine some as being more suitable than others. Stufflebeam and his associates (1985) created a table showing several procedures that might be used to gain information in order to assess "What problems are teachers having when instructing handicapped children in regular school settings?" (p. 87).

Marsh and Willis (1995) created a table illustrating several techniques useful in evaluating student achievement. It provides another perspective and offers their opinions regarding the optimal times to engage various techniques.

USING EXISTING SOURCES

There are existing sources of information about information collection procedures that administrators can refer to in order to increase their knowledge and enhance their decision-making capabilities. These resources include the Mental Measurement Yearbooks and Tests in Print, both of which should be available at large public libraries. Many standardized tests like achievement tests, personality profiles, and general aptitude tests fall into this grouping. "The advantages of measuring performance using an already existing measure are that you save time and gain the benefit of other people's experience" (Morris et al., 1987, p. 33).

ENSURING VALIDITY AND RELIABILITY

Measures that have previously been used by others generally offer information regarding validity and reliability. To be able to properly utilize these instruments, one must have a working knowledge of the validity and reliability of the results.

Gay (1992) defines validity as "the degree to which a test measures what it is supposed to measure and for whom it is appropriate" (pp. 154-155). Reliability is noted as "the degree to which a test consistently measures whatever it measures" (p. 161). Although both are important in evaluating instruments, they do not necessarily coexist. As reliability is most notably a gauge of consistency, it is possible for a test to consistently offer invalid results. "[R]eliability does not guarantee validity, although validity does guarantee some degree of reliabilityî (Hopkins et. al., 1990, p. 115). Optimally, the administrator should find instruments that are high in both as they will be the most beneficial.

ANALYZING ALTERNATIVE STRATEGIES

At this point, several possible means for collecting information have been evaluated. They differ as to the types of data they will offer. Some may be quantitative in nature; others may be more qualitative. Some information may already exist and needs only to be analyzed; some sources must be developed in harmony with the kind of information needed in a given situation; still others exist that need only to be administered to potential sources of information. Presumably, the administrator has narrowed the choices based on the situation's particularities and previous experience in selecting appropriate tools. The administrator should analyze comparatively all the strategies on this shortened list against the specific information needs and the quality and availability of the sources. "[You] will need to check that all necessary conditions exist for carrying out the activities you are considering" (Steecher and Davis, 1987, p. 15).

PRIORITIZING STRATEGIES

The prioritizing, or ranking, of strategies should take into account the costs, time, potential for bias, ease of collection, and perceived adequacy of the information collected. A matrix may be the best method to reflect accurately all of these considerations with the specific information needs. Strengths, weaknesses, and possible compromises or adaptations may become more readily apparent in this format. The variables may change from matrix to matrix, depending upon resources and needs. The main goal in creating a matrix is to be able to compare strategies available based on what is needed in a given situation. McKillip (1987) developed a matrix "containing ratings of 22 need identification techniques on 14 attributes

FIGURE 3.3. TECHNIQUES THAT CAN BE USED TO OBTAIN DATA ABOUT STUDENT ACHIEVEMENT

Techniques	Diagnostic	Formative	Summative
Informal observing and recording of student behavior	Anecdotal records *Case histories* Checklists Rating scales by teachers Unobtrusive techniques	*Anecdotal records* Case histories *Checklists* *Rating scales by teachers* Unobtrusive techniques	Anecdotal records Case histories Checklists Rating scales by teachers *Unobtrusive techniques*
Informal collecting of information from students	*Interest inventories* Rating scales by students Questionnaires Interviews *Sociograms* Self-reports	Interest inventories *Rating scales by students* Questionnaires Interviews Sociograms Self-reports	Interest inventories Rating scales by students Questionnaires *Interviews* Sociograms *Self-reports*

Analysis of examples of student work

Individual and group projects
Content analysis of workbooks
Logbooks and journals
Objective tests
Standardized tests
Essay tests
Semantic differentials
Attitude scales
Projective techniques

Testing of Students

Individual and group projects
Content analysis of workbooks
Logbooks and journals
Objective tests
Standardized tests
Essay tests
Semantic differentials
Attitude scales
Simulation and role-playing

Individual and group projects
Content analysis of workbooks
Logbooks and journals
Objective tests
Standardized tests
Essay tests
Semantic differentials
Attitude scales
Simulation and role-playing

Note: Italics refer to optimal times to use particular techniques.

FIGURE 3.4. NEED IDENTIFICATION METHOD MATRIX

Attributes for Choosing between Methods

	Resources				Analysis		
Need Identification Methods	Low Cost	Short Time	Skill Needed	Flexible	Problem-Oriented	Solution-Oriented	Relevant
1. Resource Inventory	-	--	-	0	--	++	-
2. Target Population Description	+	+	-	+	+	-	+
3. Library Research	++	+	-	++	+	+	0
4. Synthetic Estimation	+	+	-	+	+	-	-
5. Social Area Analysis	+	+	+	+	++	--	--
6. Risk Factor Analysis	+	+	-	+	++	--	-
7. Social Indicator Analysis	+	+	-	+	+	0	-
8. Client Analysis	+	+		+	0	0	+
9. Use Analysis	+	+	0	+	-	+	++
10. Barrier Analysis	-	-	0	++	++	++	++
11. Standards	++	++	+	-	--	+	--
12. Epidemiological Survey	--	--	--	++	+	+	+
13. Training Survey	-	-	++	+	-	+	+
14. Key Informant Survey	-	-	-	++	++	+	0
15. Client/Consumer Survey	-	-	+	++	+	-	+
16. Citizen Survey	--	-	-	++	+	-	--
17. Observation	--	--	++	++	+	+	++
18. Focused Group	+	0	-	++	+	+	+
19. Nominal Group	+	0	-	0	+	++	0
20. Delphi Panel	+	0	+	0	+	+	-
21. Public Hearing	--	--	+	+	+	0	+
22. Community Forum	+	0	+	+	+	-	0

Attributes for Choosing between Methods

Need Identification Methods	Analysis (Continued)			Audiences		Compatibility	
	Credi-bility	Detail	Ideas	Stake-holder	Interest	Prereq-uisites	Overlap
1. Resource Inventory	++	0	-	+	+	--	-
2. Target Population Description	+	+	+	-	-	--	--
3. Library Research	0	+	++	--	-	--	-
4. Synthetic Estimation	0	-	-	-	-	+	+
5. Social Area Analysis	+	--	-	-	-	-	+
6. Risk Factor Analysis	+	-	-	-	-	+	+
7. Social Indicator Analysis	++	-	-	-	-	--	+
8. Client Analysis	+	-	+	-	-	++	-
9. Use Analysis	++	0	+	+	-	0	-
10. Barrier Analysis	0	+	+	+	+	++	-
11. Standards	0	+	+	--	-	--	+
12. Epidemiological Survey	+	+	+	0	+	-	+
13. Training Survey	++	+	+	=	+	0	+
14. Key Informant Survey	+	+	++	++	+	-	+
15. Client/Consumer Survey	+	+	+	++	+	-	+
16. Citizen Survey	+	+	0	0	++	-	+
17. Observation	+	0	+	-	-	-	+
18. Focused Group	0	++	++	-	-	-	+
19. Nominal Group	0	+	++	+	0	-	+
20. Delphi Panel	0	+	+	-	-	-	+
21. Public Hearing	+	++	+	++	+	+	+
22. Community Forum	0	-	-	++	++	+	+

NOTE: Cell entries range from ++, indicating a criterion very characteristic of the method, to --, indicating a criterion very uncharacteristic of the method.

that are important to the choice of methods" (p. 95). It serves as an excellent example of how a matrix can aid in ranking and comparing alternatives. In McKillip's (1987) work, each need identification method is discussed in depth. An adaptation of this matrix is presented in Table 3.3.

Although this matrix does not point to one absolute best choice, it narrows the field and allows for the selection of the most valuable instrument, or instruments, given the particular situation. "The best single or combination of methods for need identification depends on the goals of the analysis and on the resources available" (McKillip, 1987, p. 98). Choosing more than one instrument, if the constraints of time and cost permit, allows for more extensive answers and precise data. It may also enhance the information that is eventually shared with others if, for example, quantifiable data regarding student's achievement were combined with qualitative case studies of the students measured.

SUMMARY

This chapter suggests that once the type of information needed is identified and fitting sources are prioritized, the selection of appropriate strategies for the actual collection of data is the next step. Sources of information relevant to the situation should be identified from what is already available, or should be developed to meet the needs of the situation. The validity and reliability of standard measures should be evaluated. All strategies still under consideration should be compared to the initial information needs and sources. A prioritization of these strategies should be developed and scrutinized; a matrix usually aids in this effort. An appropriate strategy, or strategies, if possible under the cost and time constraints, should be selected. Now the administrator is prepared for the collection process.

APPLICATION ACTIVITIES

1. You are changing the organization of the junior high school to a middle school with interdisciplinary teaching teams.

You are concerned that the community may not understand how the middle school concept works and how it will affect children. You wish to know how parents feel about the change and what they already know about middle school instruction. What strategies for gathering information from parents would you use?

2. Using the same scenario described above, what community variables would be important to consider in gathering useful data from parents?

3. Describe the role that teachers could play in strategies for collecting important information from parents on the middle school program.

4. Looking at your own school situation, how could the data collection regarding student achievement be improved?

REFERENCES

Gay, L. R. (1992). Educational research: Competencies for analysis and application, 4th ed. New York: Merrill

Hopkins, K. D., Stanley, J. C., and Hopkins, B. R. (1990). Educational and psychological measurement and evaluation, 7th ed. Englewood Cliffs, NJ: Prentice-Hall.

The Joint Committee on Standards for Educational Evaluation (1981). Standards for evaluations of educational program, projects, and materials. New York: McGraw-Hill.

Marsh, C. J., and Willis, G. (1995). Curriculum: Alternative approaches ongoing issues Englewood Cliffs, NJ: Merrill

McKillip, J. (1987). Need analysis: Tools for the human services and education. Newbury Park, CA: Sage

Morris, L. L., Fitzgibbon, C. T., and Lindheim, E. (1987). How to measure performance and use tests. Newbury Park, CA: Sage

Steecher, B. M., and Davis, W. A. (1987). How to focus an evaluation. Newbury Park, CA: Sage.

Stufflebeam, D. L., McCormick, C. H., Brinkerhoff, R. O., and Nelson, C. O. (1985). Conducting educational needs assessment. Boston: Kluwer-Nijhoff Publishing.

4

THE COLLECTION PROCESS

The educational practitioner has now completed an analysis of potential strategies and determined which of those are most applicable for the given situation. By rank-ordering possible techniques, perhaps assisted by establishing a matrix, selection of one or more is enhanced. It may better serve the confines of a particular set of circumstances to favor a combination of techniques. This approach allows for more extensive answers and more precise information once the data are actually collected. A note of caution about the use of several instruments, "Measures drawn from different data sources are not always congruent, so it may not be possible to draw desired comparisons" (Steecher, 1992, p. 79). Regardless of whether one or several strategies are chosen, an administrator should be able to collect needed information from a variety of sources utilizing a variety of methodologies. "They also must have the knowledge and skills required to direct others to seek out information" (Thomson, 1983, pp. 2-12).

When the process of actually collecting or gathering the needed information begins, it would be practicable to address several concerns. These concerns include: administering tests and measures, designing and conducting surveys, designing

and conducting interviews, making observations and recording detailed notes and behaviors, and using library sources.
This chapter will address these concerns, as well as offer some
practical examples of instruments being utilized by building
level practitioners throughout the United States. It should be
noted that a good information-collecting practitioner will also
utilize many informal devices such as chance encounters with
information holders and the news media.

ADMINISTERING TESTS AND MEASURES

The administration of tests and measurement tools is an
acquired skill and those conducting them must be able to do
so in accordance with established procedures. As is the case
with any tool, these instruments can be misused (Hopkins et
al., 1990, p. 425). There must be strict attention to detail in all
phases of the procedure, including distribution, administration, return of the instrument, and analysis of the results in
order to prevent situational characteristics from affecting the
data (see Stufflebeam et al., 1985, p. 107). Critiques of most
measurement   instruments   can   be   found   in   Mental
Measurements Yearbook. Often, as part of the instrument
package, guidelines will be suggested based on previous
implementations. When you purchase such measures you
will receive a technical manual that provides norms (if they
are available) based on the scores of a tryout group, information on the validity and reliability of the instruments, and
instructions for administering and scoring the results." If this
is not the case, then those who have used the instrument, or a
similar instrument, need to be consulted. Theoreticians at
local colleges and universities, or experienced colleagues in
neighboring districts, may be best at explaining the intrica-
cies of the instrument and its administration. John R.
Thompson, Principal of Wolcott Street School in LeRoy, New
York, wrote in a letter to the authors that the best method of
collecting information from fellow practitioners was through
e-mail and the National Distinguished Principal's Chat on
America On-Line. New technologies assist educators in seeking
out others in frank discussion of methodologies and experiences.

Gay (1992) further suggests that the administrators of existent instruments should entertain six questions as they begin:

1. Does the measure seem to be doing what it says it does?
2. How close a fit is there between the objectives of the measure and those of your program?
3. Is there information on the reliability of the measure, and is this information persuasive?
4. Does the measure seem appropriate for the age and ability level of the group you are measuring?
5. Do you have the wherewithal to do what has to be done to use the instrument?

Considering the responses to the questions, an administrator can continually evaluate the fit of the instrument being used and accommodate any unforeseen developments. Questions 1 and 2 can be evaluated as an ongoing process during the actual use of the instrument. Questions 3, 4, and 5 can generally be answered by referring to the instrument manual. If one is thoroughly familiar with the procedures listed in the manual of an instrument, then the probability of successful data collection is enhanced (Gay, 1992, p. 188). If no manual exists, as would be the case in the designing of an original instrument, consulting the manual of similar types of measurements can yield profitable guidelines.

Hopkins and his colleagues (1990) also offer these guidelines for the development of an original test or instrument of measurement:

1. Prepare a table of specifications to guide item development and selection and maximize content validity.
2. It is usually desirable to include more items in the first draft of the test than will be needed in the final form.
3. The item should be phrased so that the content rather than the form of the statement will determine the answer.
4. The difficulty level of the items should be appropriate to the group of examinees.

Item 3 should be closely adhered to as word selection may inhibit the respondents' answers. Sentence constructions that allow words like always, never, in general, exclusively, as a rule, and absolutely (p. 238) tend to undermine the integrity of the instrument. Although these guidelines were initially for test development, they present a foundation to the development of the survey inquiries.

SURVEYS

If any type of survey strategy is to be utilized, the administrator must be able to design an appropriate instrument in accordance with the needed information and mindful of the information sources. There are a variety of means possible to approach this task. Morris and her colleagues (1987) suggested a series of steps to be followed in the development of performance tests that are applicable to the development of a survey:

1. Determine the outcomes to be measured.
2. Develop a blueprint for the test.
3. Write the test items.
4. Review and edit the test items.
5. Field-test the items.
6. Obtain reliability and validity data.

Reliability and validity, as stated here, refer to the actual questions on the instrument. Do they deliver the information that they were designed to deliver? Field-testing the questions with a sample population yields valuable data as to whether the instrument being developed is accurately assessing the desired outcomes.

The method of distribution and collection must also be considered. Nuances, such as utilizing hand-outs or mailers, can profoundly affect the data collection. If a sample of parents being surveyed had the instruments brought home to them by their children, that would affect the return rate quite differently than if they had received the same instruments through the mail. Another influence would have been if the parents filled out surveys at the school of their children, perhaps while attending a parent-teacher function. Consistency must also be maintained; reliability and validity would suffer markedly if the same instrument were distributed in different methods to different portions of the survey population. The results then would be inconclusive and biased. Tim LaValley, Principal of Barnard Central School in Barnard, Vermont, in a letter to the authors, suggests attaching surveys to the school's newsletter. He explained further that the respondents should be able to complete the survey quickly and easily to ensure a higher rate of return.

Ultimate uses of a survey instrument can affect its design. The intention of this strategy to be used as a pretest, or a guide for the development of another type of measurement, would affect the very nature of the survey. This may be an advantageous use of this type of instrument as it can be an excellent means of receiving quick feedback from a sample population. If this were to be the primary use of the survey instrument being designed, there would probably be less emphasis on creating intricate questions and more focus on questions geared toward receiving general, or topical, information.

Fred Aderhold, formerly Principal at Laura Wilder Elementary and currently Principal of John F. Kennedy Elementary School, both of Sioux Falls, South Dakota, sent the authors several instruments that he has developed for data collection. Principal Aderhold utilized Quality Checks with his staff throughout the year to garner information regarding school procedures and his own performance. Two of his Quality Checks have been included here.

FIGURE 4.1. QUALITY CHECK 1

BEGINNING OF SCHOOL ACTIVITIES

Please rate the timeliness and/or effectiveness of the following items:

1 = Poor
5 = Excellent

1. Faculty letter announcing opening
   schedule of events.   1 2 3 4 5
2. Availability of class lists.   1 2 3 4 5
3. Availability of specials schedules.   1 2 3 4 5
4. Session sharing summer highlights and goals.   1 2 3 4 5
5. STAT awareness session.   1 2 3 4 5
6. One-stop sign-up table for computer, library, etc.   1 2 3 4 5
7. Time to work in rooms.   1 2 3 4 5
8. Physical conditions of your room.   1 2 3 4 5
9. Availability of supplies and materials.   1 2 3 4 5
10. Time to coordinate resources, cluster schedules.   1 2 3 4 5
11. Student assembly — rules and poster.   1 2 3 4 5
12. PTA assembled folder/handbook   1 2 3 4 5

13. Suggestions for improving the quality of beginning of school activities:

_____

_____

_____

FIGURE 4.2. QUALITY CHECK 2

BEGINNING OF SCHOOL ACTIVITIES

Please rate the timeliness and/or effectiveness of the following items:

1 = Poor
5 = Excellent

1.	Is accessible to teachers.	1 2 3 4 5
2.	Spends sufficient amount of time in the classroom.	1 2 3 4 5
3.	Consistently implements the discipline plan.	1 2 3 4 5
4.	Gives prior notice of staffings.	1 2 3 4 5
5.	Sets times & dates for evaluation and conferences.	1 2 3 4 5
6.	Communicates policy changes to staff in advance.	1 2 3 4 5
7.	Announces special events ahead of time.	1 2 3 4 5
8.	Is supportive of teachers.	1 2 3 4 5
9.	Follows up on projects and commitments.	1 2 3 4 5
10.	Publishes the weekly bulletin on Friday.	1 2 3 4 5
11.	Follows up on evaluations with the 5 day window.	1 2 3 4 5

12. Comments or suggestions that would help me to be more effective for you:

_____

_____

He also put to use a questionnaire for recent "graduates" of the elementary schooling order to determine if they were adequately prepared for middle school and to seek suggestions from those who experience the education process as students. The questionnaires are attached to a letter explaining the instruments' purpose and wishing the graduate well in their new school. These instruments are excellent examples of possible uses of a survey-style strategy.

FIGURE 4.3. SIXTH GRADE QUESTIONNAIRE

Circle the number that most closely fits your response.

5 = excellent
4 = good
3 = average
2 = not very good
1 = poor

How well-prepared were you for middle school?   1 2 3 4 5
How well-prepared were you in reading?   1 2 3 4 5
How well-prepared were you in math?   1 2 3 4 5
How well-prepared were you in science?   1 2 3 4 5
How well-prepared were you in social studies?   1 2 3 4 5
How well-prepared were you in writing reports?   1 2 3 4 5

Do you complete assignments on time?
    Always   Usually   Seldom

How do your grades at Edison compare with those at Laura Wilder?
    Better   Same   Worse

Where did you have more homework?
    Edison or Laura Wilder

How many library books have you read in the past month?
_____

What is your favorite subject at Edison?_____

How many years did you go to school at Laura Wilder?_____

Are you a male or female?   Male   Female

Did you play in the band in 5th grade?   Yes   No
Did you plan in the band in 6th grade?   Yes   No
Did you play in the orchestra in 4th grade?   Yes   No

Did you play in the orchestra in 5th grade?   Yes   No
Did you play in the orchestra in 6th grade?   Yes   No
Did you sing in chorus in 5th grade?   Yes   No
Did you sing in chorus in 6th grade?   Yes   No

What extra activities are you involved in at Edison?

_____

Suppose a new student, who is in the 4th grade, moved next door to you. That student asked you what Laura Wilder school is like. What would you tell him/her?_____

_____

What did we do at Laura Wilder that helped you prepare for middle school?_____

How could Laura Wilder staff help you be better prepared for middle school?_____

Parents: We would appreciate your comments relative to your child's preparation for middle school. We are primarily interested in students' academic training, study and work habits, and their feelings about their years at Laura Wilder.

Once again, thank you for taking time to complete this questionnaire. Your input is important to our future planning. If you have further questions or comments, please call me anytime at 332-4824.

> Sincerely,
> Fred W. Aderhold, principal

P.S. Please mail the questionnaire to:
      Laura Wilder Elementary School
      2300 South Lyndale
      Sioux Falls, SD 57105

Linda Sukkonen, Principal of Clear Springs Elementary School in Minnetonka, Minnesota, uses communication surveys in soliciting information from parents. She also has a survey that is sent to the staff in order to collect information about the performance of the school office. Principal Saukkonen provided examples of both and they are included here.

FIGURE 4.4. COMMUNICATIONS SURVEY TO PARENTS

This survey is being sent to help me gather information about communication with parents. I'd like to improve my communication to better meet the needs of the Clear Springs Community. Thank you.

1. Did you receive the monthly newsletters sent by the teacher?

     yes   no

2. Were the newsletters helpful to your understanding of the classroom?

     yes   no

3. Did you feel that the fall and spring conferences helped you to gain an understanding of your child's strengths and needs?

     yes   no

4. When you had specific questions about your child, were they answered by the teacher with promptness?

     yes   no

5. Did the teacher communicate any concerns about your child with promptness?

     yes   no

6. Was the teacher easy to reach and willing to discuss your child?

     yes   no

7. What other ways of communication and what other types of information are important for better communication between parents and teacher?

FIGURE 4.5. STAFF SURVEY

Staff,

We are collecting information about how helpful our school office is to staff. Please complete the following survey and turn it in to Linda by June 6. We will be setting improvement goals based upon your responses.

1. When you have a school problem (ex: credit, certification, payroll, ordering, etc.) is the office staff able to help you immediately or direct you to the person who can help?

1	2	3	4	5
Never				Always

    Comments: _____

    _____

2. Our policy is not to interrupt instruction unless there is an "emergency" (messages are put into mailboxes). Are you getting your messages?

1	2	3	4	5
Never				Always

    Comments: _____

    _____

3. Our intention is to give 8 hour turn around for copying at the building (ex: "In" at 8 AM, "out" at 4 PM: "In" at 4 PM "out" at 4 PM the following day). Are you getting your materials on time?

1	2	3	4	5
Never				Always

    Comments: _____

    _____

4. Does the main office staff present a warm, welcoming feeling?

1	2	3	4	5
Never				Always

    Comments: _____

    _____

5. Does the health office staff present a warm, welcoming feeling?

    _____

6. What does the office staff do well?

    _____

7. What would you like to change about the office?

    _____

INTERVIEWS

Lunenburg and Ornstein (1991), looking at the next information collection strategy from the perspective of Personnel Administration, write "probably the most widely used technique for determining what a job entails is the interview technique, and its wide use attests to its advantages" (p. 460, emphasis in the original). There are many correlations that can be drawn between interviews and surveys, but the major differences is in the nature of personally asking questions and soliciting responses.

Interviews, much like surveys, require the development of appropriate questions designed with the sources of information in mind. "School administrators who interview candidates for school positions frequently allow questions to become vague and theoretical" (Lunenburg & Ornstein, 1991, p. 476). The interviewer must avoid questions that elicit a "yes" or "no" response and attempt to draw the subject into a conversation that is reflective and honest. The responses gained should, to some degree, steer the direction of the interview and the questions that follow.

It is important for the interviewer to set aside preconceived notions and personal perspectives of the issues at hand in order to learn the true feelings and beliefs of those being interviewed. "You are not there to change views, but to learn what the subjects' views are and why they are that way" (Bogdan & Biklen, 1992, p. 99). James L. Doud, Professor and Chair of the Department of Education Leadership at the University of Florida, wrote in a letter to the authors, "those principals that I find most effective are the ones who persist beyond what appears to be verification of preconceived ideas/assumptions in an honest effort to uncover 'truth' in what is or has happened learning to anticipate many possible reasons rather than restricting our thinking to preconceived notion/causes of the problem is, I believe, a major indicator of the growth and effectiveness of a leader."

The population of interview sources may be quite similar to that of surveys, but will probably differ in the size of the sampling. Utilizing a survey as a means of developing interview questions can enhance the quality of those questions, although the reverse would also be accurate. Often, interviews yield results that can be put to use in the development of other types of measurements. Regardless, interviews allow the interviewer to gather insightful data firsthand.

The interview should be structured according to the number of the participants and whether individuals, small groups, or large groups are being interviewed. In reference to conducting need analysis, McKillip (1987) states, "Perhaps the simplest method of need analysis is to assemble a group of experts and concerned citizens and charge them with identifying the needs of the population served" (p. 86). A simple method perhaps, but one with advantages and disadvantages. In group interviews, the participants can often rouse or provoke responses from other participants. Depending on how the session is being controlled, whether a structured or more open-ended interview, these agitations can serve the interviewer well or poorly. Group interviews, large or small, can serve as a method of getting acquainted with a group that will later be interviewed one-on-one. These strategies can also serve as an introduction to certain nuances and communication strategies indicative of the group. A note of caution: the difficulties involved with conducting group interviews "include starting them and controlling the person who insists on dominating the session" (Bogdan & Biklen, 1992, p. 100). Dominating personalities are probably better suited for one-on-one interviews as they can be inhibiting and ruinous in a group setting. Phillip F. Flaherty, Principal of Westwood High School in Westwood, Massachusetts, wrote in a letter to the authors, "dominant personalities may overwhelm groups and press ideas upon more introspective people for this reason I have always made it a practice, whether or not a formal group is dealing with a question, to find time for one-one-one conversations with various interested parties."

Professor James L. Doud, in his letter to the authors, suggests using three basic questions "when involving large groups in a needs assessment process." Those questions are:

◆   What do you believe we currently are doing that is very good?

◆   What do you think we do least well?

◆   What would you like to see us doing 3 to 5 years from now that we are not doing today?

He then divides the large group into smaller groups to allow interaction and the sharing of individual responses, "eventually arriving at some type of consensus on the priorities of the group."

The design of the strategy must recognize the possible environment wherein the interviews will be conducted. In preparation for the interview, the interviewer should monitor the conditions that exist to see if they are adequate for the activities being considered (see Steecher & Davis, 1987, p. 15). Whether or not the environment is supportive, whether the questions are proffered face-to-face or on the telephone, and whether the interview is held in a classroom or an auditorium often determine the success of the procedure. Confidentiality must also be considered. "Early in the interview you try to briefly inform the subjects(s) of your purpose, and make assurances (if they are necessary) that what is said in the interview will be treated confidentially" (Bogdan & Biklen, 1992, p. 97). Gorton and Snowden (1993) consider the perspective of those being interviewed and add, "the administrator also needs to make sure that those involved understand the reason why they are being involved and the purpose, authority, and scope of their participation" (p. 24). Whatever can be done to relieve the anxieties of information sources can only aid in the collection of information.

MAKING OBSERVATIONS AND RECORDING NOTES AND BEHAVIORS

Being able to accurately record detailed notes while making observations, as a participant or not, requires skill and practice. Veit and Clifford (1985) discuss observation as a research technique and indicate that it takes "practice, concentration, and patience" (p. 191). They later suggest "copious" note taking and the writing of a report after the observation as being helpful to the process (p. 199). Documentation should include observed behaviors and nonverbal communication. Since it is difficult to write so much in such a brief period, many observers will "condense, summarize, abbreviate, and generalize" when what is truly needed is for the observer to "expand, fill out, enlarge, and give as much specific detail as possible" (Spradley, 1980, p. 68). Perhaps most difficult to do is ascribing sources for relevant quotations, or noting accurate phrasing, when in the midst of many people. One often-used method is to return to the sources and ask them to restate, to the best of their abilities, precisely what was said previously. If the intention is more toward "who" said "what," one must remember to include the context in which it was said when writing up the notes.

Ultimately, only practice and more practice will aid in the development of this skill. Seeking out others who have attempted this type of data collection can also be helpful. It remains a most difficult, but highly rewarding, form of research and source of information.

LIBRARY SOURCES

Libraries offer a wealth of resources for the collection of information. Literature searches most often begin here. Census information, financial documents, and area demographics can be tapped in the majority of libraries as well as histories and other primary sources. Often this type of information can only be accessed in a library or government office.

The library serves well those administrators who research measurement instruments prior to using them. Annual compilations of measurements, such as the Mental Measurement Yearbook, which is objectively critiqued, and Tests in Print, generally offer information on reliability and validity necessary in selecting an instrument. Journals and magazines such as Educational Researcher, Educational Administration Quarterly, Phi Delta Kappan, and many others provide insights as to how other practitioners are dealing with, and

evaluating, similar issues. Comparing a given set circumstances, or needs, with those who have attacked similar problems often reduces the amount of time administrators need to
evaluate their options.

With the advent of many forms of technology available at
such a fast rate that it is difficult to stay current, libraries often
have "cutting edge" technology long before most practitioners.
Libraries usually have a large database such as the National
Educational Longitudinal Study of 1988, Children's Reference
Plus, High School and Beyond, and the Longitudinal Study of
Youth. There are excellent sources of tremendous amounts of
information, often utilized by practitioners and educational
researchers. Searching ERIC, The Educational Resources and
Information Clearinghouse, is probably the best starting place
for any practitioner venturing into the field of research. Data
regarding legal issues in education can be obtained in any
well-maintained law library, or if the library carries Lexis, by
accessing up-to-date computerized information. Services such
as computerized literature searches and abstracts of previous
research can assist the administrator and reduce the time nor-
mally involved in ambitious projects.

The simple sharing of the problem at hand with a librari-
an who is knowledgeable of the field and research methods
can greatly benefit the educational practitioner and narrow
the focus of the process. If a library cannot answer specific
information regarding research and data collection, then it
remains the best resource for directing the investigation of
any practitioner.

This chapter was geared toward the collection process. The
key concerns addressed included: Administering tests and
measures, designing and conducting surveys, designing and
conducting interviews, making observations and recording
detailed notes and behaviors, and using library sources. The
chapter also includes examples of instruments used by building level practitioners throughout the United States, which is
the next step in analyzing collected data.

APPLICATION ACTIVITIES

1. If you have designed a survey instrument that parents will be asked to complete, what are several strategies that you would use in ensuring that parents receive and return the instruments to the school?
2. Describe ways that small group interviews might be used in your school to improve communication and information gathering by the principal.
3. Design a survey instrument that would be useful to you regarding community perceptions of the school and its relationship to the needs of the community.
4. What are the informal means for information collection that might be useful to the school principal beyond the typical informal conversations and observation?

REFERENCES

Bogdan, R. C., and Biklen, S. K. (1992). Qualitative research for education: An introduction to theory and methods, 2nd ed. Needham Heights, MA: Allyn & Bacon.

Gay, L. R. (1992). Educational research: Competencies for analysis and application, 4th ed. New York: Merrill.

Gorton, R. A., and Snowden, P. E. (1993). School leadership and administration: Important concepts, case studies and simulations, 4th ed. Madison, WI: WCB Brown & Benchmark Publishers.

Hopkins, K. D., Stanley, J. C., and Hopkins, B. R. (1990). Educational administration: Concepts and practices Belmont, CA: Wadsworth.

Lunenburg, F. C., and Ornstein, A. C. (1991). Educational administration: Concepts and practices. Belmont, CA: Wadsworth

McKillip, J. (1987). Need analysis: Tools for the human services and education. Newbury Park, CA: Sage.

Morris, L. L., Fitzgibbon, C. T., and Lindheim, E. (1987). How to measure performance and use tests. Newbury Park, CA: Sage.

5

INFORMATION ANALYSIS

Effective gathering of high-quality information is an important component of the information process. However, presenting or discussing such data in the absence of sound conceptualization and analysis may produce results that are difficult to comprehend at best; at worst, they can be misleading and subject to misinterpretation by the principal's constituency and stakeholders. Within the politicized context in which schools currently exist, it is important that principals work to minimize the possibility of such misconceptions. Accordingly, reliable information conceptualization and analysis is critical to successful gathering and dissemination of information. Broadly, initial information analysis includes conceptualization, categorization, and organization of data, management of data, and inspection of these data to determine relationships among them.

DEVELOPING CATEGORIES FOR CLASSIFYING INFORMATION

Although there are a number of ways to think of data and to organize them into categories, we will present here two rel-

atively straightforward ways to organize data to aid in understanding them. Each has its own different uses, strengths, and
weaknesses. The first strategy involves developing categories
in advance of data collection. This a priori strategy can guide
administrators in making decisions on types of data that they
need to gather and the types of instruments to use. Examples
of a priori category development might include dropouts vs.
participators, high achievement vs. low achievement, attitude
toward school, etc. In each of these examples, the administrator would have chosen these categories prior to information
collection to meet a particular need or interest of the school
system. If this strategy is used, categories should be opera-
tionalized carefully so that the meaning and boundaries of
each category are clear. Without clear delineation of categories,
agreement on data collection targets may be difficult to obtain,
and results of data collection are more likely to be difficult to
interpret. An a priori strategy is simplest and most useful
under the following conditions: (a) data to be gathered are primarily quantitative; (b) provision for data collection has been
made early in the planning process; (c) categories of interest
are relatively discrete and straightforward; and (d) categories
are already available from the literature, policy, or experience.

A second categorization strategy is to develop classes of
information following examination of existing data. This strategy is particularly useful in the absence of predefined categories, where planning for evaluation has not occurred, and
with qualitative data. For example, educational programs
often are implemented with little specification of desired outcomes. When evaluating these programs for purposes of funding or accountability, specific categories of outcomes may have
to be developed from existing information from the programs.
In addition to lowering dropout rates, a dropout prevention
program might have as actual, yet unspecified, objectives that
include increasing achievement, improving participation,
developing more positive school attitudes, etc. In the absence
of predetermined categories such as these, the administrator
may need to examine available data to decide what is important, desirable, or available as indicators of program outcomes.

Another example might be development of student categories from existing records. In this case, specific student group characteristics may not be available, even though a considerable amount of general data are within easy access. Careful examination of such data often reveals patterns of information associated with types or groups of students (e.g., dropouts, at-risk students) that can yield meaningful categories for program development or policy formulation. Because this categorization procedure may be somewhat more subjective than development of categories from predetermined sources, care should be given to triangulation and confirmation of categories by independent raters or additional sources of information. In this way, reliability of categories can be maximized and errors of classification can be minimized. Although this type of categorization may be more subjective than the a priori strategy presented above, data resulting from organization and categorization of existing information often are easier to interpret than predetermined categories. Also, they frequently are more meaningful to participants in the schools who must respond to and utilize such data in the classroom.

CREATING A MANUAL OR COMPUTERIZED MANAGEMENT INFORMATION SYSTEM TO FACILITATE INFORMATION RETRIEVAL

When information from surveys, questionnaires, and interviews begins to come in, it can quickly become so voluminous and complex that it is difficult to manage. To keep control of the data and to facilitate their examination, it is helpful to develop an organizing system that also will serve to distill the data into uniform units of analysis. Although such systems typically are computer-based, text-based (or even picture-based, etc.) strategies may be effective to manage and study categorized information. For the purposes of this chapter, computer-based strategies will be the primary management system of interest.

Prior to entering data into a computerized information

management system, it is important to develop an organizing framework to guide data entry and to facilitate subsequent retrieval of information. This framework typically is codified into a text-based document called a manual or codebook. The manual consists of a list of categories or variables, an abbreviated name to be used for each category or variable in the computer program, and a brief description or definition of each category or variable. Each manual should reflect precisely the nature and contents of the available data. The manual represents a centralized organizer and description of the contents of the database to be developed from the raw data, and is an important and useful tool in managing and communicating the contents of the database. However, developing an effective manual requires an in-depth understanding of the categories that organize the data, as well as the ways that they relate to each other. Due to the importance of this step to the overall process, we encourage principals to develop the manual carefully and, if needed, to practice with different manual organizations to determine the best way to manage data once they are entered. In this way, data organization can be "debugged" prior to computer data entry, and the principal can gain valuable understanding of underlying data structures and possible interrelationships. A simple example of a data manual is presented in Figure 5.1.

Following data gathering and development of the manual, data entry typically occurs. Several computer program options are available for this step, each of which has its strengths and particular applications. If the data are primarily numeric and data analyses will be mostly descriptive (e.g., means, standard deviations, simple correlations), then spreadsheet programs such as Lotus 1-2-3, Microsoft Excel, or Quattro Pro are appropriate tools for data organization and analysis. If the data are primarily narrative and data analyses will be mostly descriptive (e.g., frequencies), then database management tools such as dBase, Paradox, or Microsoft Access are excellent programs for organization and analysis. However, if the data are primarily numeric and complex statistical analyses (e.g., multiple linear regression, factor analysis) are needed, then statistical

FIGURE 5.1. SAMPLE MANUAL

Variable Name	Variable	Variable Description
	Teacher Demographics	
TID	Identification Number	
TAGE	Age	YY=years; MM=months
TSEX	Gender	1=Female 2=Male
TRACE	Race/ethnicity	1=African American 2=Latino 3=American Indian 4=Caucasian
TDEG	Degree level	3=Doctoral 2=Masters 1=Bachelors
	Student Demographics	
SID	Identification Number	
SAGE	Age	YY=years; MM=months
SSEX	Gender	1=Female 2=Male
SRACE	Race/ethnicity	1=African American 2=Latino 3=American Indian 4=Caucasian
SSES	Socioeconomic status	1=Free lunch program 0=Not eligible for free lunch program
SGRADE	Grade level	

analysis programs probably are the most appropriate tools. These include such programs as SAS and SPSS. Finally, data that are primarily narrative and are to be analyzed for themes and commonalities may require specialized data analysis programs such as Ethnograph or Q.S.R. NUDIST, which are designed for inspection of qualitative and narrative data. A heuristic table summarizing these ideas is presented in Figure 5.2.

FIGURE 5.2. HEURISTIC RULES FOR CHOOSING TYPES OF COMPUTER PROGRAMS FOR DATA ANALYSIS

If data are primarily:	and the intended analysis is:	Then use:
Numerical	Mostly descriptive	Spreadsheet programs
	Complex statistical	Statistical analysis packages
Narrative	Mostly descriptive	Database programs
	Contextual or thematic	Specialized narrative analysis programs

A CASE STUDY

A case study will be presented here to illustrate an information analysis process. The case study presented involves an information gathering procedure in the public schools related to at-risk students and academic failure. Because diverse procedures are available and effective in executing such activities, it should be noted that the example described below provides only a single instance of data conceptualization and analysis. We encourage educational practitioners to explore creative ways to examine data.

Pilot At-Risk Interventions with Rural Schools. Rural schools often lack service delivery options and community alternatives to meet the complex needs of at-risk children. Pilot At-Risk Intervention with Rural Schools (PAIRS) was a grant-funded project developed to fill this need (Short, Meadows, & Moracco, 1992). The PAIRS project was a partnership between three rural Alabama school systems, the Alabama Governor's Office on Substance Abuse Policy, the Alabama Department of Education, and Auburn University to develop a comprehensive school-based model for serving at-risk youth. The goals of the project were: (a) public schools in the project would increase their ability to identify and serve at-risk children; (b) coordination of services between public schools and community-based service providers would increase; and (c) the needs of students receiving services through the project would be met.

A central task of the PAIRS project was to develop a school-based decision-making mechanism for evaluating data, planning interventions, and coordinating resources. At its outset, this task required the development of an efficient, valid, reliable, and fair method of identifying children at risk of school failure before they had suffered significant school failure. Because risk factors in school failure have been identified in recent legislation and literature as being multidimensional, the method of identification needed to reflect the multiple determinants of risk, while minimizing the effect of labeling. School principals and teachers from each school worked to develop multidimensional procedures to identify at-risk students. These procedures included review of cumulative records, teacher nomination forms, and self-report measures. School principals and teachers at all project schools were responsible for developing the content, format, and administration approach for data gathering. Subsequently, all schools administered and analyzed the procedures they developed.

An initial step in conducting the process described above was to think through the concept of at-risk and the types of information that might be needed to operationalize it. The principals and teachers had access to recent state and federal legislation and policy statements related to the topic, wherein were listed general characteristics of at-risk students from the policy perspective. These lists constituted the schools' initial conceptualization of risk factors related to academic failure. With the help of the university, school personnel also surveyed the literature on at-risk students to get information on additional dimensions of risk that might be important, and the principals and teachers also brought ideas from their own experience concerning risk factors peculiar to their schools. From these various sources, each school developed a comprehensive base on information about at-risk students, from which they extracted a list of variables related to risk and academic failure. These lists were discussed through several meetings to yield a smaller list of risk factors that was applicable to the school in which it would be used. The importance of this step needs to be emphasizedówithout an adequate understanding of the construct being studied by the school, including categories of information that comprise it, subsequent activities may produce results that are difficult to understand or explain.

Following identification of relevant factors, each school discussed possible sources to be used to provide information about each one. Among others, these sources included archives, school discipline records, teacher reports, absentee reports, tardy reports, parent information, grades, and student reports. School principals and teachers identified sources of information that seemed best for measuring the level of risk related to the factors identified in the previous step, with attention to using multiple sources whenever possible. For example, both teacher reports and formal discipline reports were used to assess levels of disruptive behavior. From this matrix of risk factors and information sources, project schools developed a systematic procedure for data gathering and analysis. A sample PAIRS matrix is presented in Figure 5.3.

For the purposes of this chapter, we will present a single component of such a matrix from one of the project schools. In this school, the principal and teachers chose to use a teacher survey as one measure of the level of risk factors associated with academic failure in their school. Thus, the team used a school data source (teacher surveys) to identify risk factors across all dimensions of risk for academic failure. Although such a strategy is efficient and relatively easy to implement, it must be remembered that teacher surveys constitute only a single data source for assessing risk factors. The questionnaire used for the school described above is presented in Figure 5.2.

FIGURE 5.3. SAMPLE PAIRS RISK DIMENSION/INFORMATION SOURCE MATRIX

Risk Dimension/ Information Source	Child Sources	Family Sources	School Sources	Community Sources
Child risk factors	Self report; Observation; Interview	Parent interview; Parent survey; Behavior checklist	Grades; Attendance records; Teacher reports; Discipline records	Reports from community residents and leaders; Community survey
Family risk factors	Survey or checklist; Interview; Focus groups	Parent self-report; Observation	Teacher survey; Teacher interview; Cumulative record review	Community participation analysis; Reports from community leaders
School risk factors	Attitude toward school survey; Participation analysis; Interview	Parent survey; Parent interview, Focus groups	Analysis of school rules; School organization analysis	Reports from community leaders; Focus groups of community residents
Community risk factors	Environmental survey; Interview	Parent participation analysis; Parent survey; Parent interview	Educator report; Records of school-community contact; Free lunch percentage	Community survey; Analysis of census data; Epidemiological studies

FIGURE 5.4. PAIRS TEACHERS CHECKLIST

Check each item that applies to the student. This form is to be used only for early detection or a student who may potentially be at-risk of failing or dropping out of school, and to be used only as a guide for assessment.

(1 = not at all a problem; 7 = very much a problem; DK = don't know)

	1	2	3	4	5	6	7	DK
Parent(s) did not finish high school	1	2	3	4	5	6	7	DK
Language problems	1	2	3	4	5	6	7	DK
Frequent absences or tardies	1	2	3	4	5	6	7	DK
Previous suspension or expulsion	1	2	3	4	5	6	7	DK
Higher-than-average rate of discipline problems	1	2	3	4	5	6	7	DK
Low achievement test scores	1	2	3	4	5	6	7	DK
Low school grades	1	2	3	4	5	6	7	DK
Repeated one or more grades or required courses	1	2	3	4	5	6	7	DK
Severe reading problems	1	2	3	4	5	6	7	DK
Poor study and work habits	1	2	3	4	5	6	7	DK
Alienation from and disinterest in school	1	2	3	4	5	6	7	DK
Unstable home environment	1	2	3	4	5	6	7	DK
Socially isolated	1	2	3	4	5	6	7	DK

Poor interpersonal/social skills	1 2 3 4 5 6 7 DK
Lack of positive peer relationships at school	1 2 3 4 5 6 7 DK
Frequent physical and emotional problems	1 2 3 4 5 6 7 DK
Low self-concept, low self-esteem	1 2 3 4 5 6 7 DK
Alcohol or drug abuse (includes underage use of tobacco)	1 2 3 4 5 6 7 DK
Low level of participation in extracurricular activities	1 2 3 4 5 6 7 DK
Short attention span	1 2 3 4 5 6 7 DK
Easily victimized	1 2 3 4 5 6 7 DK
Victimizes other students	1 2 3 4 5 6 7 DK
Inability to face pressure	1 2 3 4 5 6 7 DK
Fear of failure	1 2 3 4 5 6 7 DK
Easily influenced	1 2 3 4 5 6 7 DK
Changes in dress, hygiene or weight	1 2 3 4 5 6 7 DK
Non-English or limited English language background	1 2 3 4 5 6 7 DK
Insufficient support services (e.g., counseling, remedial)	1 2 3 4 5 6 7 DK
Lack of self-discipline	1 2 3 4 5 6 7 DK

Examination of the instrument shows that risk factors of concern to the school are listed on the left side of the page, and teachers were asked to rate the presence and extent of each factor for each child in his or her class. Questionnaires contained no provision for student names or other identifying information. Surveys were distributed to teachers for their completion and returned anonymously to the principal's office. Data from the survey provided information about teachers' perceptions on a number of critical risk factors associated with their school. In aggregate, these data provided a picture of risk at the school, and provided significant information to guide school-level and school-community intervention planning. Taken with other sources of data such as student perceptions, archives, and parent perceptions, the instrument provided a useful planning and policy tool for the principal and for the school.

It is important to note here that the questionnaires were structured to avoid any type of identifying information about individual students. The purpose of the survey was to gather information about school-level risk factors, rather than information on individual children. Data gathering of this type on individual students should be done carefully and only with parental consent. There is a considerable danger of such information resulting in labeling of children who are experiencing academic difficulties as being "at-risk," potentially causing lowered expectations and other school difficulties. Although identification of at-risk students is important for targeted interventions, early stages of prevention and intervention often benefit from more general information about school characteristics, as opposed to individual student characteristics.

Using the ideas presented at the beginning of this chapter, schools participating in the PAIRS project used the at-risk literature and their own experiences and expertise to develop an a priori system for understanding characteristics of students at risk of failing in school. With this framework, they developed multiple ways of gathering information to help them grasp the nature and extent of the problem within their schools. Categories of information developed from their work provided them an important tool for organizing the data they collected into a database with which they could assess needs, measure progress, and identify continuing concerns. One possible way of setting up such a database is presented in Figure 5.3.

Data gathered from interviews of teachers and parents and observations of schools and classrooms also provide useful information in another way. By conducting qualitative analyses of these data to uncover spontaneously occurring themes and patterns in participant perceptions and behaviors, administrators are able to uncover important contextual clues that often remain unnoticed with the use of more quantitative strategies. Careful examination of narrative data from interviews and observations, sometimes with the aid of computerized qualitative analysis programs, provides interesting information about participant views, concerns, and reactions. Additionally, qualitative strategies allow data gatherers to account for the richness and complexity that are natural characteristics of schools, yet often escape notice in a priori and quantitative strategies. By systematically collecting, synthesizing, and interpreting narrative accounts of interviews and observations, trends and patterns of events, interactions, and outcomes can be reliably ascertained. Conclusions drawn from such analysis often are quite useful in understanding and intervening within particular settings, as opposed to uncovering general findings about broader settings. For example, teacher interviews in School A might yield a consistent pattern of concern about parent involvement that does not appear in the PAIRS teacher survey, and therefore would not be addressed if only the teacher survey was used. Narrative data from teacher interviews also might uncover additional real-life patterns in school A, such as typical outcomes or antecedents associated with particular risk factors.

A specific example of a qualitative strategy to gather information related to the above matrix would be an analysis of barriers to academic success from several different perspectives. Teachers, administrators, and parents could be asked the open-ended question, "What barriers to learning do you see in School A?" Responses to this question could be transcribed, analyzed to determine specific themes, and coded on these

FIGURE 5.5. SAMPLE DATABASE OF RISK FACTORS BY SCHOOL

	School A	School B	School C	School D	School E
Parent(s) did not finish high school	3.1				
Language problems	2.4				
Frequent absences or tardies	5.2				
Previous suspension or expulsion	5.0				
Higher-than-average rate of discipline problems	6.4				
Low achievement test scores	6.0				
Low school grades	6.6				
Repeated one or more grades or required courses	4.1				
Severe reading problems	3.7				
Poor study and work habits	2.9				
Alienation from and disinterest in school	3.3				
Unstable home environment	5.9				
Socially isolated	2.4				

Poor interpersonal/social skills	2.3				
Lack of positive peer relationships at school	3.0				
Frequent physical and emotional problems	2.0				
Low self-concept, low self-esteem	2.3				
Alcohol or drug abuse	2.6				
Low level of participation	4.5				
Short attention span	5.2				
Easily victimized	2.7				
Victimizes other students	3.1				
Inability to face pressure	2.0				
Fear of failure	2.2				
Easily influenced	2.6				
Changes in dress, hygiene or weight	1.9				
Non-English or limited English	1.9				
Insufficient support services	4.8				
Lack of self-discipline	4.0				

themes to ascertain common and unique factors related to academic failure. These factors could be corroborated using school records, child reports, and available community data. In this way, barriers could be identified flexibly from participant perspectives and validated by archival data, without assuming that particular barriers are present based on literature reviews or surmises. This approach has the additional benefit of involving participants in thinking about academic problems and solutions.

Schools participating in these activities gained substantial and powerful information about their schools in a way that provided clear targets for intervention. Additionally, they developed procedures and instrumentation for future data gathering and analysis. Perhaps most important, however, was that they became quite sophisticated in recognizing at-risk factors and in judging methods of gathering data. All these skills made the principals and teachers more knowledgeable about their schools, but also more expert in data gathering and analysis. With adequate attention to theory and previous research, any problem can be addressed effectively by using the simple, yet comprehensive, approach described above. These problems may be sufficiently divergent to include gang problems, meeting the expectations of future employers, or academic performance.

SUMMARY

In this chapter we have discussed procedures for setting up information analysis, including conceptualization of the data and how they will be analyzed. These initial steps are crucial to effective information processing, and dovetail well with subsequent activities around more in-depth data analysis and reporting. In the next chapter, we will discuss ways on understanding and reporting the information gathered in this process.

APPLICATION ACTIVITIES

1. Develop a list of factors that you think are associated with some issue that is presently an important topic in your school system, such as dropping out or retention. Think about how the factors might be represented in a data set and set up a codebook for entering them into a computer.
2. Using a computerized database or spreadsheet program, set up a dummy data set for your variables.
3. Find a set of data in your school system and decide which computerized data storage program you should use.

REFERENCES

Fits-Gibbon, C. T., and Morris, L. L. (1987). How to analyze data. Newbury Park, CA: Sage.

Isaac, S., and Michael, W. B. (1984). Handbook in research and evaluation. San Diego, CA: EDITS.

Short, R. J., Meadows, M. E., & Moracco, J. C. (1992). A project to meet the needs of rural at-risk children: Pilot At-Risk Interventions in Rural Schools (PAIRS). In R. C. Morris (Ed.), Solving the problems of youth at risk: Involving parents and community resources. Lancaster, PA: Technomic, pp.176-180.

6

UNDERSTANDING THE INFORMATION

To make further sense of the information collected, principals must summarize and describe it. This chapter provides an overview of tools for comparing data and investigating relationships among them. Also, the chapter discusses ways of understanding and reporting quantitative and qualitative information to consumers.

ANALYZING QUANTITATIVE INFORMATION

Quantitative information, once gathered, may seem overwhelming in the sheer mass of numbers with which principals have to deal. Fortunately, a number of procedures are available to facilitate distillation of the information into manageable units, searching for relationships among the numbers, and reporting these relationships. Two of the most basic of these procedures are the mean and the standard deviation. Both of these statistics are necessary for analyzing and understanding numerical information, and also are fundamental building blocks of more complex statistical procedures described below. The mean of a group of numbers essentially is nothing more than their average, calculated by adding up the numbers and dividing by how many numbers are in the set. For example, the mean of the number of absences for five children that have

5, 6, 4, 7, and 2 absences, respectively, for the year is (5+6+4+7+2)/5, or 4.8. Knowing the mean for a particular group allows meaningful comparisons of individual scores, characteristics, or performances to the average number for the group-to determine whether the individual score is above average or below average. Knowing the average number of absences in the above example allows us by comparison to conclude that the first child has an above-average number of absences (5 of them), while the third child was absent a below-average number of times (4 absences). However, knowing the mean does not allow us to ascertain how far above or below average an individual score is. This is important in determining more precisely the relative positions of numbers in relation to the average. To know this, we must know and understand the standard deviation.

Simply stated, the standard deviation is a measure of how spread out from the mean a set of scores are. The larger the standard deviation, the more spread out the scores are (that is, the greater the variance); the smaller the standard deviation, the more packed in around the mean the scores are. Conceptually, the standard deviation is nothing more than the average of the distances from the mean of all scores in a set. The formula for a standard deviation is:

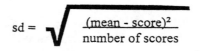

$$sd = \sqrt{\frac{(mean - score)^2}{number\ of\ scores}}$$

Although this formula looks complicated, just remember that the standard deviation really is nothing more than how far from the mean (in standard units) a score is. If you know the mean and standard deviation of any group of numbers, you can determine exactly how high (or how low) each score is with respect to the mean. The mean of any distribution is at the 50th percentile — it's right in the middle — and the first standard deviation always accounts for about 34% of the distribution above and below the mean. Thus, one standard deviation above the mean is always at about the 84th percentile (50 + 34) and one standard deviation below the mean is always at about the 16th percentile (50 - 34). The next standard deviation out from the mean always accounts for about an additional 14% of the distribution. Two standard deviations above the mean would always be at about the 98th percentile (50 + 34 + 14), and two standard deviations below the mean would always be at about the 2nd percentile (50 - 34 - 14). And so on. If you know the mean and standard deviation of a group of numbers, you can plot the exact position of each number with respect to the mean.

As will be described below, this knowledge can directly translate into a standard score such as an IQ or SAT scale score, or can be converted easily into a percentile rank. In the example above with a mean of 4.8, the standard deviation formula provided can be used to calculate an sd of approximately 1.7. A score of 6.5 (that is, 4.8 + 1.7) is one standard deviation above the mean, and a score of 3.1 (or 4.8 - 1.7) is one standard deviation below the mean. We know, then, that a score of 5 is just above the 50th percentile, and a score of 7 is higher than more than 84% of the set of numbers. It's just larger than 6.5, which is one standard deviation above the mean, or at the 84th percentile.

At perhaps the easiest level of data representation, principals can use simple frequencies to display and understand their data. Frequencies involve simple counting of instances of particular phenomena, such as absences, number of games, parent visits, etc. Frequencies are much more interesting and useful when they are collected for different categories and then compared with each other. For example, number of absences in a school district is much more useful when separated out into number of absences for each school or for each grade level. In this way, particularly meritorious or problematic schools or grade levels can be identified. To determine whether differences across categories can be explained by chance, some statistical test (see Table 6.1) is often useful. Also, frequency-by-category data may be more readily interpretable using graphs and charts. Figure 6.1 provides an example of such a representation.

FIGURE 6.1. A BAR CHART OF ABSENCES FOR FOUR SCHOOLS

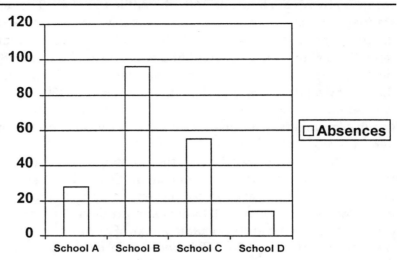

Following conceptualization of the data-gathering process, information gathering, and data entry (described in previous chapters), quantitative data typically are manipulated using a computerized analysis package. If data analysis needs are simple or text-based, database management or spreadsheet programs generally will suffice to conduct needed breakdowns. However, more sophisticated analyses typically require dedicated statistical packages, such as SAS or SPSS. A list of common statistical procedures for data analysis, adapted from Isaac and Michael (1984), is presented in Table 6.1.

It is beyond the scope of this book to provide in-depth coverage of statistical techniques that may be useful in understanding relationships in the data. For this reason, we encourage principals to work with local or nearby universities to secure needed statistical expertise in analyzing data.

INTERPRETING QUANTITATIVE INFORMATION

Using quantitative data suggests that we are measuring some characteristic or unit of interest to us. Accordingly, understanding of quantitative data requires a good grasp of principles of measurement, which is simply assigning num-

FIGURE 6.2. COMMON STATISTICAL TECHNIQUES TO
ANALYZE RELATIONSHIPS IN DATA

Technique	Description
Simple correlation	Measures the degree of relationship between two variables.
Partial correlation	Measures the relationship between two variables when additional variables are present. These additional variables are held constant.
Multiple correlation	Measures the relationship between a dependent variable and some combination of predictor variables.
Factor analysis	Investigates patterns of interrelationships among a large number of variables. Provides a smaller number of dimensions to account for these interrelationships.
z-Ratio or t-Ratio	Tests whether two samples came from the same population or are different from each other.
Analysis of variance	Tests whether several groups, possibly at several levels, came from the same population or are different from each other.
Chi-square	Determines whether frequencies of numbers in categories differ from each other.

bers according to rules (Fits-Gibbon & Morris, 1987). Viewed this way, measurement essentially comprises three broad areas of concern: the types of numbers to be assigned, how the numbers (scores) can be given additional meaning, and how good the numbers are at measuring that meaning (Fits-Gibbon & Morris, 1987).

Assigning Numbers. Any measurement can be done at one of four levels, or scales. Each level, or scale, is more complex than its predecessor and allows for more comprehensive manipulation and use of analytic techniques. These levels are described below.

1.   *Nominal scale.* Nominal scales consist of numbers assigned to units to represent names, categories, or types of information. In nominal scales, different numbers do not represent different quantities; rather, they represent different categories — the numbers serve as names. For example, religious affiliation could be coded by assigning numbers to religious categories (e.g., 1 = Protestant, 2 = Catholic, 3 = Jewish, etc.). Another example, common in the schools, is student ID numbers. Because these numbers function as names, they cannot meaningfully be added, subtracted, multiplied, or divided.

2.   *Ordinal scale.* Ordinal scales place units in an order according to the degree to which they possess a trait or characteristic. For example, ordinal scaling would be used in ordering children in a classroom in terms of reading ability from first to last, or in a study of teachers' values, asking teachers to rank 10 values from most important to least important. Although ordinal scaling is somewhat more sophisticated mathematically than nominal scaling, it provides no information about the distance between values of the scale; that is, the difference between any two points on the scale may not be equal to the difference between any other two points. Ordinal scaling allows only the determination that one value is more than another.

3.   *Interval scale.* Interval scaling also places units in an order, but in such a way that the distances between numbers assigned to them are equal. For example, the difference between 400 and 500 on the verbal section of the SAT is the

same as the difference between 600 and 700:100 SAT points. However, interval scaling remains limited in that it cannot be said sensibly that a student who scores 800 on the SAT verbal is twice as smart as another who scores 400. This is because interval scaling does not define a zero point — an SAT score of 0 doesn't mean no verbal ability.

4. *Ratio scale.* Ratio scaling is the same as interval scaling, but adds a natural zero point. This addition allows ratio comparisons to be made between scores. For example, height in inches is a ratio scale because height has a zero value, so it can be said that one person is twice as tall as another.

Because categories on a nominal scale represent only qualitative differences between categories, they cannot be manipulated mathematically in any meaningful way. Ordinal scaling allows for some comparisons (e.g., less than, more than), but cannot be used to calculate averages or manipulated with other common statistics in education. If arithmetic or statistical analysis is necessary, data should be gathered at least at the interval level.

Giving Scores Meaning — Interpreting Individual Scores on a Measure. Through the use of tests and other instruments, numbers associated with each procedure can be assigned to individual students, teachers, administrators, schools, etc. These numbers are called raw scores. As an example, the at-risk instrument presented in Chapter 5 consisted of a series of items on a 7-point scale from 1 (not at all a problem) to 7 (very much a problem). The scale used here is called a Likert-format scale, and is assumed to be an interval-level scale. For purposes of determining a general level of risk, all the items could be summed across the instrument to yield a single at-risk score. Obviously, higher scores would indicate greater risk. However, it would be impossible at this point to judge how much risk is normal or at what level of risk we should be concerned about students or schools. Is a raw score of 20 a dangerously high level of risk? Should we be concerned that school A has an average score that is 10 points higher than school B? Without additional information, raw scores are sufficiently difficult to interpret so that questions such as these cannot be answered meaningfully. However, raw scores can be converted to standard scores to allow comparisons to provide at least partial answers to these questions.

A *standard score* is a transformation of raw scores that takes into account the mean and standard deviation of the group. When a test developed by a test publisher is used in your school, the standard scores given to your students use the means and standard deviations of a large sample (a test standardization sample). There are several different, but related, types of standard scores. A z score is a standard score that provides the deviation of a raw score from the mean in standard deviation units; the distribution of z scores is set up to have a mean of 0 and a standard deviation of 1. As you will remember, standard deviation is the degree of spread, or variation, in a distribution of scores for a group. The larger the standard deviation, the more heterogeneous the group on the trait measured.

Use of standard scores provides a means of comparison that allows for answers to questions like the ones listed above. If the calculated mean for the at-risk inventory is 25 and the standard deviation is 5, then an obtained score of 20 is one standard deviation below the mean, a z score of -1. At least within the context of the larger group, then, a raw score of 20 actually represents a significantly low level of risk. A z score is -1,which is 1 standard deviation below the mean, represents the 16th percentile of the group surveyed. Knowing the z score of any school or student allows a judgment about the level of risk in comparison to the reference group by providing a frame of reference for interpreting an individual score. The z score expresses how far above or below the mean the individual score is. Assuming a normal, bell-shaped distribution, an assessment of the percentile rank of the individual score also is possible.

Several other standard scores are commonly used in educational assessment and research, most of which merely are transformations of z scores to make them easier to work with. T scores are another kind of standard score used to avoid the minus signs and decimals involved in z scores. By definition,

T scores assign a score of 50 for the mean and 10 for the standard deviation; however, a T score of 50 is exactly the same as a z score of 0, and a T score standard deviation of 10 is exactly the same as a z score standard deviation of 1.

Other standard scores include IQ scores (mean of 100 and standard deviation of 15) and SAT and GRE scores (mean of 500 and a standard deviation of 100). Although the means and standard deviations of these various standard scores seem radically different from each other, the important thing to remember is that, regardless of the number assigned to them, the mean is always at the middle and the standard deviation is always the same distance from the mean. One way to think of standard scores is to compare them to different temperature scales. Even though different numbers get assigned to the freezing point for water, the actual freezing point stays the same. Having a stable freezing point allows us to compare different scales effectively. In a similar way, having standard scores allows us to compare across tests and individuals effectively.

Several other ways of conceptualizing and reporting data are commonly used in education. These include percentile scores or ranks and grade equivalency scores. Percentile scores or ranks are statements of the percentage of individuals in the large sample a given person exceeds. For example, a score at the 99th percentile equals or exceeds the scores of 99% of the people measured, and 50th percentile means that at the mean, 50% are at or below the score obtained. Although percentiles are easy to report and seem easy to understand, they are only at the ordinal level of measurement. This makes differences between percentiles difficult to interpret and explain successfully to constituents.

Grade equivalents provide the grade level for which the individual's score is the real or estimated average. For example, a grade equivalent score of 6.4 indicates that the person tested scored as the average child in the 4th month (of a 10-month school year) of 6th grade scored or would score. Again, grade equivalent scores seem intuitively attractive and easy to understand. However, these scores, which appear to give information about the actual mastery of the curriculum at a particular grade level, actually only indicate performance comparative to the average student performing at that level. Curriculum mastery cannot be ascertained through grade equivalent scores. Another problem is that grade equivalent scores don't represent an interval level scale. Unfortunately, these scores can easily be misinterpreted by the school to the parents, though the original impetus for their use probably was to communicate in a concrete way to parents.

A CASE STUDY (CONTINUED)

To illustrate some of the points made in this chapter, we will use the example of the PAIRS project presented in the previous chapter. The teacher questionnaire described in Chapter 5 provided quantitative information about a number of risk factors that were relevant to the schools in the project. These data were entered into a computerized database and simple statistical analyses were conducted to determine means and standard deviations for each risk factor. These results are presented in Table 6.3.

By themselves, these numbers seem difficult to interpret except at the most rudimentary level. For example, we can determine by visual examination that discipline problems, low achievement test scores, and low school grades seem to be highest on the list. However, at least one of them, low achievement test scores, has a very high standard deviation. This suggests that there was considerable variation in teachers' perceptions of the occurrence of this factor in their students. Also, it is impossible to ascertain through visual inspection whether frequent absences or tardies belong in this high group, or whether they are really a little lower than they are in the teachers' perceptions. The best way to investigate for real differences among the factors is to use statistical techniques on a computer. In this case, using T-tests to conduct a series of pairwise comparisons would provide information about significant differences among the factors, so that principals could discern which factors are indeed the most problematic and in need of intervention.

FIGURE 6.3. MEANS AND STANDARD DEVIATIONS
FOR RISK FACTORS IN SCHOOL A

Factor	Mean	Standard Deviation
Parent(s) did not finish high school	3.1	1.5
Language problems	2.4	.6
Frequent absences or tardies	5.2	1.1
Previous suspension or expulsion	5.0	.9
Higher-than-average rate of discipline problems	6.4	1.7
Low achievement test scores	6.0	2.9
Low school grades	6.6	1.0
Repeated one or more grades or required courses	4.1	.7
Severe reading problems	3.7	1.5
Poor study and work habits	2.9	1.4
Alienation from and disinterest in school	3.3	2.0
Unstable home environment	5.9	2.1
Socially isolated	2.4	1.3

Poor interpersonal/social skills	2.3	.8
Lack of positive peer relationships at school	3.0	1.0
Frequent physical and emotional problems	2.0	.7
Low self-concept, low self-esteem	2.3	1.6
Alcohol or drug abuse (includes underage use of tobacco)	2.6	2.1
Low level of participation in extracurricular activities	4.5	1.2
Short attention span	5.2	2.0
Easily victimized	2.7	.9
Victimizes other students	3.1	1.8
Inability to face pressure	2.0	1.0
Fear of failure	2.2	.8
Easily influenced	2.6	1.5
Changes in dress, hygiene or weight	1.9	1.4
Non-English or limited English language background	1.9	1.2
Insufficient support services (e.g., counseling, remedial)	4.8	2.0
Lack of self-discipline	4.0	1.3

To investigate which of the factors on the questionnaire are most related to academic failure and to determine the particular configuration of variables that best predicts academic failure, a multiple regression analysis can be conducted. Using this procedure, academic grades from cumulative records (or whatever criterion of academic performance is most useful) could be used as the criterion variable — what the school wants to predict. The factors on the questionnaire would constitute the predictor variables — what the school wants to use to predict the criterion variable. The multiple regression analysis should provide information about the relationship of each factor to academic grades (simple correlation), how much each factor is related to academic grades when other factors are included (partial correlation), and which pattern of factors, taken together, is most related to academic grades (multiple correlation). In this way, principals can have information about interventions for which factors might have the most effect on academic grades, along with the previously mentioned information on factors that teachers rated as being most prevalent in their students. Both of these types of information should provide considerable advantage in planning interventions. In fact, PAIRS schools found that to be just the case!

Other potential uses: Scores of individual students and measuring change. At least two additional uses might be made of the information gathered from the questionnaire, although great care should taken (and additional analyses carefully undertaken) to ensure that the questionnaire measures reliably what it was designed to measure. Should the questionnaire be determined to have good psychometric properties (adequate reliability, validity, fairness, and norms), it may be useful as a screening tool to identify students in need of additional services before they begin to experience significant failure. Use of the instrument for this purpose would require conversion of factor raw scores into standard scores for both the student's scores and the group means to allow for easy and meaningful comparison (see interpretation section above).

A second possible use might be to measure school-level

change in level of risk factors at some later time. This might provide some data for evaluation of intervention programs designed to lower specific risk factors in the school. Again, conversion to standard scores would facilitate comparisons and promote understanding in presentations of information to constituents. As an example, we can examine changes in levels of risk factors from the PAIRS instrument at the beginning of the school year and again at the end of the school year, after project interventions were put into place. Results of these administrations are presented in Table 6.4 on page 112.

Simple visual inspection of the respective means indicates a rather dramatic decrease in ratings of several risk factors. These include absences and tardies, suspensions, discipline problems, low participation, and insufficient services. Although most of the other risk factors remained about the same, a few actually increased over the intervention period. These include poor work habits, fear of failure, and difficulty with pressure. Whereas visual inspection can yield interesting surmises (particularly when differences are large), real differences (those not occurring due to chance) in pretest-post-test scores can only be uncovered through statistical analysis. In this case, a series of T-test comparisons of the pretest and post-test mean for each risk factor might be used to ascertain which, if any, of the risk factors really changed over the course of the intervention. Because large numbers of comparisons increase the likelihood of obtaining significant results that are due to chance, some type of control for Type I error (finding results that really are due to chance) may be needed.

INTERPRETING QUALITATIVE INFORMATION

Although quantitative data analysis is important to the process of data-based administrative decision making, it cannot answer all the questions that may interest educators and administrators. Whereas quantitative data analysis may address questions of why and how much (which deal with prediction and measurement), questions of how (which address understanding) are more appropriately explored through qualitative techniques. An example of educational issues that might reflect this question is "How do decisions get made in school-community meetings?" and "How do teachers come to be socialized into a school's organizational climate?" or even "How do children solve social problems?" The answers to these questions are more concerned with understanding complex events than with testing hypotheses, with describing process rather than outcome, and with examining perceived or constructed reality rather than objective reality.

The strength of qualitative data analysis lies in its emphasis on systematically gathering data, with minimal constraints, in the natural setting. It focuses on understanding the subjective and objective relationships between phenomena within a setting. By avoiding the reduction of data into numerical terms, ethnographic research seeks to develop a rich, holistic, integrated picture of events and participants.

Qualitative data gathering and analysis is a systematic, empirical approach to knowledge acquisition that uses many of the investigative tools that educational practitioners use on a daily basis. These techniques include methodical observation, interviews, and review of records and historical data. Although quantitative data are not necessary to conduct qualitative research, they are not antithetical to the method and may be used to complement and support qualitative findings. These techniques are used within a research framework that consists of a broad definition of general problem dimension or research area. Thus, observations, interviews, records reviews, and quantitative measurements are structured toward understanding some broad phenomenon of interest to the principal. In contrast to quantitative research method, the investigator maintains flexibility in the type and extent of data to be gathered to answer research questions. In working to answer research questions, the goal of qualitative research is understanding. The qualitative data analyst seeks to deal with issues of alternative explanations for phenomena (handled in quantitative research by experimental and statistical control) by being open to and investigating all possible explanations of phenomena in the setting of interest.

These explanations are discovered by a systematic exami-

FIGURE 6.4. MEANS AND STANDARD DEVIATIONS FOR RISK FACTORS
IN SCHOOL A BEFORE AND AFTER INTERVENTION

Factor	Mean1	SD1	Mean2	SD2
Parent(s) did not finish high school	3.1	1.5	3.1	1.6
Language problems	2.4	.6	2.2	1.0
Frequent absences or tardies	5.2	1.1	2.3	1.9
Previous suspension or expulsion	5.0	.9	3.9	1.2
Higher-than-average rate of discipline problems	6.4	1.7	5.0	1.6
Low achievement test scores	6.0	2.9	5.8	2.9
Low school grades	6.6	1.0	6.1	1.5
Repeated one or more grades or required courses	4.1	.7	4.2	.9
Severe reading problems	3.7	1.5	3.9	1.3
Poor study and work habits	2.9	1.4	3.7	2.0
Alienation from and disinterest in school	3.3	2.0	3.0	1.6
Unstable home environment	5.9	2.1	5.8	2.2
Socially isolated	2.4	1.3	3.0	1.4
Poor interpersonal/social skills	2.3	.8	2.7	1.1

Lack of positive peer relationships at school	3.0	1.0	2.5	.7
Frequent physical and emotional problems	2.0	.7	2.7	1.9
Low self-concept, low self-esteem	2.3	1.6	2.5	1.5
Alcohol or drug abuse (includes underage use of tobacco)	2.6	2.1	2.4	1.6
Low level of participation in extracurricular activities	4.5	1.2	3.0	1.1
Short attention span	5.2	2.0	5.1	1.8
Easily victimized	2.7	.9	3.0	1.1
Victimizes other students	3.1	1.8	3.0	1.7
Inability to face pressure	2.0	1.0	2.9	1.4
Fear of failure	2.2	.8	4.3	1.1
Easily influenced	2.6	1.5	2.5	1.3
Changes in dress, hygiene or weight	1.9	1.4	1.5	1.5
Non-English or limited English language background	1.9	1.2	1.9	1.1
Insufficient support services (e.g., counseling, remedial)	4.8	2.0	2.3	1.4
Lack of self-discipline	4.0	1.3	3.3	1.8

nation of data to discover trends and consistencies among data. In contrast to quantitative data analysis, examination of data to ascertain trends begins at the onset of data collection. Qualitative data analysis comprises three stages that are cyclic and begin at data collection. The first of these stages is data reduction, which includes distillation of large amounts of complex data into smaller, reliable units. Data reduction often occurs with the aid of computerized narrative analysis tools, as mentioned in the previous chapter. The second stage is data display, which involves representing qualitative data in multiple ways that maximize interpretability and understanding while maintaining integrity of the original data. The final stage is verification and conclusion-drawing, which involves checking of assumptions and interpretations against multiple data sources for consistency and integrity, and combining data into defensible inferences to facilitate understanding.

As an example of qualitative analysis, let us examine the question of how decisions are made in parent-teacher association meetings. Although this area might be studied using surveys or other quantitative techniques, such techniques may fail to capture important relationships in and details of the process of PTA meetings. Further, quantitative techniques may lack sufficient flexibility to allow for changes in research emphasis to capture critical, but unexpected, occurrences. Accordingly, a qualitative design may be the best tool for gathering and analyzing data to answer questions about this area of school functioning.

As an initial data-gathering step, several PTA meetings could be observed by trained researchers, who would make extensive field notes about characteristics of the meetings. These notes might include such dimensions as who attended the meeting, who spoke at the meeting, how the meeting room was organized, and other possibly important facets of the meetings. Additional data in the form of interviews of participants would be gathered. Participant interviews could be structured around a broad interview outline that solicits information on participant perceptions of how decisions are made, who makes decisions, and the effectiveness of PTA decision making. Finally, archival records in the form of meeting minutes might be examined to determine the types of decisions reported in records of meetings.

All three types of data, observations, interviews, and archives, could be transcribed and examined for broad themes or categories of data. Analysis of the relationship of these themes to each other, as well as determination of common themes across PTAs and themes that are unique to individual teams or subgroups of teams, represent an important part of qualitative analysis. Consistency of themes across data sources also provides for checks on integrity of data sources and data gathering. After identifying and analyzing themes among the various data sources, conclusions drawn from the data can be checked by comparing them across data sources as well. Gathering and analyzing data in this manner can provide a rich, detailed picture of the decision-making process in PTA meetings. Such information might then be used to guide principals' decisions concerning parent involvement, allocation of resources, and other critical facets of school-community relations.

SUMMARY

In this chapter we have described some ways of summarizing and presenting information. We presented broadly a number of statistical analysis procedures, as well as provided a basic introduction to understanding and presenting quantitative information and qualitative data. In many cases, both numerical information and narrative data are very difficult to interpret in their raw forms, necessitating manipulation and distillation to uncover important comparisons and relationships. Often, such manipulation is beyond unaided human analysis, and computer aids typically are used to allow more powerful examination of information. Computer-based statistical analysis may require additional expertise and should be planned for in advance whenever possible. We recommend exploring development of relationships between schools and nearby colleges or universities to secure this expertise.

APPLICATION ACTIVITIES

1. Design a data analysis procedure that uses each of the four scales of measurement. To ensure that your procedure is understandable to others, give specific examples of each procedure.
2. Using a survey you have developed for exercises in a previous chapter or (better yet) some assessment procedure you have used in your practice, compute means and standard deviations for the raw scores. Convert the raw scores to one of the types of standard scores.
3. Interview several of your colleagues on some current topic in your school system, such as teacher pay, extended school year, etc. Audiotape the interviews or take careful notes and transcribe them into a narrative. Examine the narrative transcriptions to see if you can uncover some common concerns, observations, or perceptions among the interviewees.

REFERENCES

Fits-Gibbon, C. T., and Morris, L. L. (1987). How to analyze data. Newbury Park, CA: Sage.

Goetz, J. P., and LeCompte, M. D. (1984). Ethnography and qualitative design in educational research. San Diego, CA: Academic Press.

Isaac, S., and Michael, W. B. (1984). Handbook in research and evaluation. San Diego, CA: EDITS.

Patton, M. Q. (1980). Qualitative evaluation methods. Beverly Hills, CA: Sage.

Schein, E. H. (1987). The clinical perspective in fieldwork. Newbury Park, CA: Sage.

Short, R. J., Meadows, M. E., and Moracco, J. C. (1992). A project to meet the needs of rural at-risk children: Pilot At-Risk Interventions in Rural Schools (PAIRS). In R. C. Morris (Ed.), Solving the problems of youth at risk: Involving parents and community resources. Lancaster, PA: Technomic, pp. 176-180.

Van Maanen, J. (1983). Qualitative methodology. Beverly Hills, CA: Sage.

7

SOME FINAL THOUGHTS ON INFORMATION COLLECTION AND IMPLICATIONS FOR PRINCIPALS

This book has provided an introduction to an important component of data-based administrative decision making: information collection. Information collection sometimes is a complex and time-consuming activity, but there is no substitute in the overall process of data-based decision making. Without information collection, problem solving is limited to surmise and opinion. Because information collection can be complex, we recommend working with local or regional universities to get additional help in accomplishing this step. However, the information in the previous chapters should provide a framework from which information collection can proceed.

Several general implications can be drawn from the material presented in this book. These implications may be valuable to administrators as organizing principles in their efforts to collect and understand information for decision making, or they may serve as starting points for additional reflection and study of the evaluation and problem-solving process. In any event, the following points serve to summarize our thinking on information collection for decision making.

1. It is important for principals to have data available to them for decision making. As we noted earlier, reliable and valid data are always needed to support and verify identification of needs, to back up the administrator's position with his or her constituency, and to answer critical questions of practice that accrue to the administrator's functioning. Effective administrators make informed decisions, based on consistent and

trustworthy knowledge. Although good information doesn't guarantee effective decision making, the lack of such data severely limits both conclusions and options.

2. Effective information collection requires careful planning. Because it often is time-consuming and somewhat intricate, data collection is often difficult to manage when it is casually conceptualized and implemented. Under these conditions, well-meaning efforts may fail to be carried out or may result in unproductive or uninterpretable findings. Information collection should be conceptualized and planned well in advance of decision making and should be systematically put into place. In fact, the best time to think through information collection may be at the very beginning, rather than at the end, of any program planning process.

3. Information collection should be driven by decision needs, not by available instruments, data, or measures. Administrators should take care to identify the types of data and measures that will answer the questions most relevant to their decision making. Following this identification, decisions can be made about the availability of existing instruments versus the need to develop measures and procedures to answer pertinent questions. Although it is tempting to define practice questions in terms of available measures to save time and effort, this strategy often results in failure to address specific questions that are critical to the problem situation. Using canned instruments or data may cause a subtle shift from the original needs and focus of the investigation.

4. Parents, students, and community members are excellent sources of information. Particularly when decisions to be made are concerned with perceptions, attitudes, and values, stakeholders are important information sources. However, even data-based information (e.g., grades, curfews, etc.) can be gathered veridically from key informants. An additional benefit of collecting information from the community, parents, and students is that it creates the impression of openness to their ideas, opinions, and suggestions. Used this way, information collection can create a positive climate and

increase stakeholder investment in the decision-making process. Also, periodic focus group interviews with students in the school can provide important information regarding students' perceptions of the effectiveness of the school, how well the school is meeting needs, and areas for improvement.

5. Local and regional universities and community agencies may be able to provide resources to design and develop instruments for data collection. In addition to measurement expertise that is often available at universities, outside institutions may be willing to provide valuable collaborations and additional types of expertise to the school. These added facets will have long-term benefits for the school and the administrator in terms of additional resources and contacts. As in the previous point, such contacts also increase university and community investment in decision making.

6. To ensure effectiveness, administrators should budget for information collection. Although data collection may not require massive expenditures to be adequate for decision making, the activity seldom can be undertaken realistically without some consideration of funding. Following definition of data needs and types of measures, costs of instruments and procedures should be investigated and reported realistically. Sufficient funds should be allocated to ensure gathering of high-quality information for decision making.

7. Partnerships with business and industry can provide resources for information collection. Community businesses often conduct surveys and collect other data to facilitate their own decision making. Especially for purposes of conducting an environmental audit for the school, local and area businesses may be willing to help administrators with data collection as part of their own information collection. In many cases, the information collected will be useful for both parties in their planning and will provide avenues for subsequent sharing and collaboration.

Appendix

FIGURE A.1. PARENT SATISFACTION

Dear Parent,

Please take a moment to let us know how we're doing. Continuing with this issue of the newsletter, there will be periodic surveys to give you the opportunity to let us know how you feel about how things are going at Laura Wilder. The following questions deal with the Fall Fair, Cherrydale Farms fund raiser and parent-teacher conferences. Please circle your responses, write any comments and return to your child's classroom teacher. Thank you for your participation.

Please return by December 7.   Fred Aderhold, Principal

HOW SATISFIED WERE YOU WITH THE FOLLOWING ITEMS?

Excellent = 5   Poor = 1 Not Applicable = NA

FALL FAIR

Convenience of the date and time of the carnival.	5	4	3	2	1	NA
Change of menu from pizza to spaghetti.	5	4	3	2	1	NA
Games and activities.	5	4	3	2	1	NA
Should we continue to have a Fall event?	5	4	3	2	1	NA

Do you think we should try a different family-type event   YES   NO

Suggestions or ideas for other events to bring families together _____

Comments or suggestions about the Fall Fair. _____

CHERRYDALE FARMS FUND RAISER

Quality of the products.	5	4	3	2	1	NA
Price of the products.	5	4	3	2	1	NA
Selling and ordering procedures.	5	4	3	2	1	NA
Pick-up of items.	5	4	3	2	1	NA

Would you purchase or support this fund raiser next year?   YES   NO

Do you have suggestions for other types of fund raisers?

PARENT-TEACHER CONFERENCES

Convenience of date and time of conferences.	5	4	3	2	1	NA
Conference schedule information.	5	4	3	2	1	NA
Helpfulness of the office in rescheduling.	5	4	3	2	1	NA
The conference format, i.e., 15 minute schedule	5	4	3	2	1	NA
The value of your conference.	5	4	3	2	1	NA
Principal is accessible at conference times.	5	4	3	2	1	NA
Feel welcome to call or stop in and talk with principal with questions or concerns.	5	4	3	2	1	NA

Comments or suggestions to improve parent-teacher conferences:

Circle the grade level of your child   K   1   2   3   4   5

FIGURE A.2. PARENT SATISFACTION

Dear Parents,

Please take a moment to let us know how we're doing. Beginning with this issue of the newsletter there will be periodic surveys to give you the opportunity to let us know how you feel about how things are going at Laura Wilder. The following questions deal with the start of the new school year. Please circle your responses, write any additional comments and return to your child's classroom teacher. Thank you for your participation.

Please return by Oct. 12.   Fred Aderhold, Principal

HOW SATISFIED WERE YOU WITH THE FOLLOWING ITEMS?

Excellent = 5   Poor = 1 Not Applicable = NA

	EXCELLENT				POOR	

THE FIRST DAYS OF SCHOOL:

1. Pre school letter informing of child's teacher assignment	5	4	3	2	1	NA
2. Information included in the above letter about the start of school, i.e., start times, where to meet teacher, etc.	5	4	3	2	1	NA
3. Pack of information in the take-home folders.	5	4	3	2	1	NA
4. Parent/student handbook (printed inside front of take-home folders).	5	4	3	2	1	NA
5. Instructions on forms to fill out and return to school were clear.	5	4	3	2	1	NA
6. Information on bus schedules prior to start of school.	5	4	3	2	1	NA

OPEN HOUSE:

7.	Format of the Open House.	5	4	3	2	1	NA
8.	Day and time of the Open House	5	4	3	2	1	NA
9.	The Newcomers' Orientation	5	4	3	2	1	NA

PLEASE RESPOND TO THE FOLLOWING QUESTIONS:

1.	Are you new to Laura Wilder?	YES	NO
2.	Are you new to Sioux Falls?	YES	NO
3.	Does your student ride the bus?	YES	NO

What suggestions might you have to improve the start of the school year?

_____

Did your child have any comments or reactions to the first days of schools?

☐ Check here if you would like someone from school to contact you.

Name and phone number: _____
(Optional)

FIGURE A.3. KINDERGARTEN ASSESSMENT

_____   _____   _____
  (Child's Name)   (School Year)   (Teacher's Name)

Codes: Red: 1st nine weeks   Blue: 2nd nine weeks
              Green: 3rd nine weeks   Black: 4th nine weeks

Alphabet: Upper Case
__A __B __C __D __E __F __G __H __I __J __K __L __M __N
__O __P __Q __R __S __T __U __V __W __X __Y __Z

Lower Case
__a __b __c __d __e __f __g __h __i __j __k __l __m __n
__o __p __q __r __s __t __u __v __w __x __y __z

Numbers: recognize numbers
__1 __2 __3 __4 __5 __6 __7 __8 __9 __10

Numbers: meaning
__1 __2 __3 __4 __5 __6 __7 __8 __9 __10

Shapes:

◯   ☐   △   ▭

__   __   __   __

Fine Motor Skills:
__Tie shoes   __Cuts with control

Prints: __First   __Last

__Identifies left/right

Gross Motor Skills:
__Hops   __Skips   __Jumps

Can State:
__Telephone#   __Address   __Poems   __Days of the week

__Enjoys singing

Comments:
_____

_____

FIGURE A.4. THIRD MIDTERM PROGRESS REPORT. RALEIGH ROAD SCHOOL

MONTH _____ 19__

NAME: _____ TEACHER: _____

CODE: N - Not yet S - Sometimes Y - Yes M - Most of the time

SOCIAL/EMOTIONAL DEVELOPMENT
1. Shares and takes turn   _____
2. Works carefully   _____
3. Follows rules and classroom procedures   _____
4. makes good use of time   _____

PHYSICAL DEVELOPMENT
1. Shows large muscle development as circled.
                    throws   catches
2. Shows small muscle development as circled.
                    ties snaps buttons zips
3. Has control when using:
   scissors
   crayons
   pencils

MATH
1. Recognizes and understands numerals as circled:
   0 1 2 3 4 5 6 7 8 9 10
2. Matches sets and numerals as circles:
   0 - 5   6 - 10

LANGUAGE
1. Listens attentively
2. Recognizes letters as circled:
   Aa Bb Cc Dd Ee Ff Gg Hh Ii Jj Kk Ll Mm
   Nn Oo Pp Qq Rr Ss Tt Uu Vv Ww Xx Yy Zz
3. Can state:
        Telphone number   _____
        Address   _____
        Days of the week   _____

COMMENTS _____

Conference Needed ____Yes ____No
*Please sign and Return white copy to teacher

_____
Parent Signature/Date

FIGURE A.5. INSTRUCTIONAL SUPPORT TEAM PROCEDURE
BERNARD CENTRAL SCHOOL

The Instructional Support Team (IST) is a collaborative effort to provide strategies for working with all children effectively.

PURPOSE: The goal is to assist every teacher in meeting the needs of his or her students by sharing staff skills and creating opportunities to improve staff communication in the areas of instruction and classroom management.

GOALS: Instructional Support Team (IST) members will work collaboratively to provide assistance and services for teachers. This assistance/service may be provided through any of the following activities:

> Brainstorming
> Help in development of materials
> Coaching
> Demonstration Teaching
> Observations
> Implementation Instruction
> Behavioral Management Strategies
> Validating Teacher Actions
> Providing Suggestions for Interaction
> Recommendations for In-Service Training

TEAM MEMBERS SHALL INCLUDE:

1.   Principal
2.   Primary Classroom Teacher
3.   Intermediate Classroom Teacher
4.   Special Education Teacher
5.   School Psychologist, Guidance Counselor, Nurse, and/or other special area teachers will be involved as needed.

The referring teacher may choose to bring any additional staff who may be of help in discussing the child in question (i.e., last year's teacher, Chapter 1 teacher, etc.).

MEETINGS: Meetings should be scheduled regularly once a month.
Interim meetings may be requested by a teacher when
deemed necessary.

RECORD KEEPING: Summary forms will be kept in Individual Student File. At each meeting a secretary will be designated to record the minutes. Meeting minutes will be retained by the Guidance Counsel.

Recognition of a Problem   The teacher identifies a student concern which manifests itself in some type of school-related difficulty, or the problem may be identified through group testing, or by a parent or other students.

Individual Assistance   The teacher devises a plan for working with the pupil to help overcome the problem. The teacher may request help from the principal or other school support staff. Parents may be notified of the problem through a parent/teacher conference and may be asked to assist in resolving the problem.

Request for Additional Assistance   The teacher prepares the referral form (see attached) and documents attempt to meet the student's needs. This form should be submitted to the Principal.